New Economy
Self-Development Series
Volume I

Life in a Rapidly Changing World

Pauline Tai

ISBN: 0-75961-536-5

This book is printed on acid free paper.

1stBooks – rev. 05/21/02

**For
Christine, Kirsten
and
Michael
With love**

Table Of Contents

vi

Preface

Being a good student, as many recent university graduates have discovered the hard way, is no guarantee of a challenging career or a satisfying life. The reason: what's being taught in our current educational systems can actually be a hindrance to getting a good job, building a successful career and developing a fulfilling life.

"The kind of abilities that get you 'A's' in courses are minimally overlapping with the kind of abilities that make someone successful on the job, and that's the problem," says Robert Sternberg, IBM professor of psychology and education at Yale University. "The point is that no matter how smart you are in a traditional school sense, if you don't have the basic practical smarts, you can't get anywhere; even in the so-called ivory tower of university, no one wants to hire you."

The purpose of this series of four little guides of about 100 pages each is to give high school and college-bound students a starting point in developing some of these "basic practical smarts" that will help them make an easier transition from dependents to productive-earners and taxpayers in the future. This first volume covers some of the key survival basics that are needed to make the most of the new economy. It is in effect a quick introduction to the real world of work. Its main goal is to help them gain some insight and understanding of how an evolving economy can affect their lifestyle and what they can do to minimize the often, painful effects of these on-going, irreversible structural changes that are increasingly accompanied by volatile cyclical upheavals.

The remaining three guides will cover the four areas that play a pivotal role in life: education and career in second volume, personal finance in the third and personal history in the fourth. Although part of a series, each volume is a complete entity by itself, and can be read separately or chronologically as a whole. Even the chapters are self-contained so they can be treated like individual articles in a magazine. The choice then is entirely up to the reader's own interest at any particular point in time.

Although this series is written especially for young adults, two other groups may find them informative and useful as reference guides:

(1) Recent graduates and workers forced into redundancy or early retirement may find some useful tips from these guides. For many in Asia, who have prospered beyond their dreams in the last few years, the recent economic crisis has been a much-needed wake-up call. The longer the after shock persists, the greater its effects will be. For the next few years, China too will be traversing a rough patch as the central government carries out its plans to close many of its money-losing state-owned enterprises. Millions of workers will lose their jobs. Unlike previous eras when jobs were assigned by the government, they will now have to fend for themselves. During periods of such prolonged economic uncertainties, there is always a growing demand for information on survival, self-development and personal finance.

(2) Parents and teachers may also find these books of interest. Not so very long ago, when extended families were the norm, there were always other adults around who would act as surrogate parents. As a result, most children had the daily care and support from not only their parents, but also a host of other relatives and servants. Today, most families live in small, nuclear units with just the children and the parents. Whether it is to make ends meet or simply to satisfy one's own destiny, often both parents are working full time today. As a result, many children feel neglected, even though they may have live-in nannies. What they lack is consistent parental guidance and discipline in their daily life. Also, an increasing number of families are headed by single parents, the majority of whom are women with low-paying jobs.

According to a recent survey of Hong Kong children, their on-going chief complaint about their parents is the lack of time they have with them. Their one wish to their parents: allow more time both to talk and listen, as well as to do things together. No doubt this is a common wish for children everywhere in the world today, where often for economic advancement or survival, both parents must work long hours outside the home.

Of course parents too have their own concerns and problems. But in the daily struggle of balancing the needs of their family and making a living, they often compromise by neglecting their own private needs. With the rapid advancements in technological innovations in recent years, many have also found it difficult to keep up with all the changes that are happening. We are confused and in need of help to understand our changing circumstances and environment. How can we help our children, if we ourselves don't fully understand what is going on?

Little books with big thoughts

One of the greatest pleasures I get out of my work as a financial reporter is the opportunities it gives me to chat with people from all walks of life about what concerns and bothers them. Being a generalist at heart, it was natural that whether I was working at the Wall Street Journal, Money or elsewhere, I would get many of the more unusual calls and letters from our readers. As a result, I've had lots of opportunities to find out what's on their mind. Interestingly, it's not only the common folks who need help but also the experts. Often all they needed was a source to contact to get all the facts. Or, more common still, someone knowledgeable and willing to listen to what is confusing them.

With this series, you too can take advantage of what I learned by being a sounding board. In this age of the Internet, it is ironic that while an immense amount of information is now more readily available and at a much lower cost than ever before, locating relevant and useful material with practical applications is still a time-consuming, exacting task. The purpose for these guides is to weed out the excess and present you with just the basic facts and background information so you'll get a firm handle of the concepts involved and develop a better sense of how things relate to each other. Having this knowledge will help you to sort out the many options you will face to arrive at solutions that fit your own needs.

This series of self-development guides have three unique features:

(1). Take what is happening in the world and reported in the news and interpret why these major economic events affect common people's everyday life and livelihood. Perception is one thing, but reality can sometimes be something else entirely. The fine line between myth and fact can often be blurred or simply erased as special interest groups vie for a shrinking pool of resources.

(2). Give tips and suggestions on what we as workers, consumers and investors can do to prepare and help ourselves to cope in this increasingly uncertain and volatile environment.

(3). As most trends in recent years begin in the United States, where needed, these guides will use U.S. case studies to illustrate how things have panned out and what lessons, if any, we can learn from them. Up to now, most financial and tax books tend to be regional rather than global in scope — the result of publishing tradition and factors such as different laws, regulations and practices in different countries. For such books to be relevant for this Internet age, where borders are increasingly blurred or erased, they must take a more universal approach. For readers to get a complete picture, these books must cover in some details three major areas:

▶ **The basic concepts** — how things function in theory.
▶ **The reality** — how things work in a political, social and economic environment; history, tradition and cultural differences may all have some effect.
▶ **The strategies** — what individuals need to do to build a constructive and fulfilling life in this new world.

Most of us have some idea of the reality — if not completely, we at least know what it may be, as much of this is included in the daily news coverage. What we lack is some historical perspective that will help us to understand and relate what is happening in the larger world to our own place in it. Having a firm foundation on these basics will promote self-confidence and result in a stronger self-identity. Without a good grounding on the concepts and our recent history, it's quite impossible to deal with the reality and develop the strategies that are needed to survive in this fast-evolving world. As timeliness and interaction are crucial for dealing with the reality and strategies, these two will be more effective, if presented in an on-line environment such as the Internet.

This series of four guides will concentrate almost exclusively on the universal truths that apply everywhere no matter where we may live in the world. To put things in perspective, where necessary, some background or history will also be included. These little books will also ask lots of questions to make you think and, hopefully, understand how things apply to you personally. In short, these are step-by-step guides to knowing yourself. They're like concise road maps, where the direction and routes are clearly identified and marked, but it is still up to you to pick the specific path that will lead you to the next leg of your adventurous journey through life.

As you embark on your exciting, exploratory trips into the new economy, I hope you'll find these guides an informative and helpful traveling companion. Drop me a line, if in your journeys you have any thoughts that you'd like to share with me. Bon voyage!

Acknowledgments

Through the years, I have interviewed numerous money managers and other financial, education and career experts. I've also had ample opportunities to chat with people of all ages from all walks of life about what concerns and delights them. I have learned much from them. Many of these same people contributed most generously in time and patience to make this self-development series a reality. A good number of them also read the manuscripts for accuracy. For their interest and time, I thank them from the bottom of my heart.

I'd also like to thank those friends and family members who took the time from their very hectic schedules to read the manuscripts and made many useful suggestions. I thank, in particular, Rosemarie, who did everything from designing the books, to double checking facts, to making sure the PCs and other equipments are functioning efficiently; Tom and Margaret, who shared with me their technical expertise. Last but certainly not least, I thank Ed, Amy and Kirsten, who spent precious vacation days querying, editing and proofreading the manuscripts with great care and clarity.

Hong Kong   **P.T.**
   2001

Foreword

The book you have before you was foreordained. Author Pauline Tai possesses a unique blend of qualities that made it inevitable that she would write this highly useful, extremely accessible survival guide to the new economy. Those qualities: an abiding interest in young people, a truly multicultural perspective and a solid grasp of how the world works.

I have known Ms. Tai as a friend and colleague for two decades, through several professional incarnations and on more than one continent. She and I first worked together at Money Magazine in New York, and we attended the same fellowship program at Columbia University – a program she went on to direct. We have dined together at the Foreign Correspondents Club in Hong Kong, and we have even bunked together in Connecticut, where we were on assignment and the local motel had only one vacant room left.

Ms. Tai brings to this book and series long experience as a teacher and a financial journalist. She also brings worldliness – in the best sense of that word. Born in China and educated in the United States, Ms. Tai speaks five languages and divides her year among Asia, Europe and the U.S.

Her book begins with a reality-based tour of the world's rapidly evolving economies, one that assesses the trends toward globalization, privatization, consolidation and deregulation, as well as the revolutionary changes sparked by high technology and the Internet. That would be accomplishment enough, but Ms. Tai goes on to examine the impact of these epic trends on readers' lives. She offers readers practical help with weighing their strengths and weaknesses and hard-headed advice on thinking independently, maintaining an open mind, and developing a positive attitude. She inventories the skills that will be of paramount importance in the years to come – computer literacy, multilingual fluency and a mastery of the basics of economics.

When it comes to economics, Ms. Tai is on home turf and the tutorial she delivers here is first rate. She retraces the economic history of the past twenty years and provides a comprehensive review of definitions and concepts.

Lastly, she identifies the most valuable resources available, both in print and on-line, in areas ranging from education, to career, to personal finance and more.

In sum, Ms. Tai has produced in about 100 pages, nothing less than the first fine installment of an owner's manual for anyone with a brain.

Caroline Donnelly
Editor-in-Chief
Family Money Magazine

New York
2000

1. A changing world: the challenges and the perils

Introduction

With the dawn of a new millennium, it is time for celebrations as well as for reflections about the past and, more importantly, what to expect for the future. When the cold war ended in the late 1980s with the fall of the Berlin Wall and communism in the former Soviet Union, there were cheers and expectations about a new world order. Although more than a decade has now elapsed, we have yet to figure out what that phrase really means in practical terms. However, we do see some major shifts in priorities around the world that are sure to leave long-lasting imprints on the way we will live and work in the coming decades.

During the cold war era, geopolitics played the major role in world affairs. Today it's economics and trade that hold the key. This switch has unleashed further momentum in the rapid advancements in technology, market innovations and deregulation. As globalization and digital technology take hold in the 1990s, these processes are accelerating at an even faster pace. In such a super-charged milieu, where the world's financial markets are increasingly being driven into unfamiliar terrain, traditional rules and practices simply don't apply any more.

As economies become industrialized, the manufacturing sector tends to decrease in importance, paving the way to the growth of the service industry and more recently to e-commerce or whatever else that's connected with the Internet. In this new economic and social environment, the traditional mode of earning a living is being eroded. Until recently, most people work in jobs that produce goods in order to earn money to live. As heavy manufacturing requires a good amount of investment up front to get started, only those with sufficient capital and assets to borrow funds were able to have their own businesses.

Today we have a growing segment of the population who don't really work in the traditional sense any more. These can be divided into two broad categories: those who start Web-related businesses and those who play the stock markets. Most anyone with a personal computer and some interest in the Internet can now start their own business, as witnessed by all the young entrepreneurs turned multimillionaires or multibillionaires in only the past few years. According to the 1999 annual Forbes survey of the richest Americans, of the 60 new names that year, 35 are billionaires and 19 have fortunes derived from Web-related businesses.

Those who make a living playing the markets include individual investors, speculators and a growing contingent of "day" traders, who churn the markets by hopping in and out of shares daily. An increasing number of people from all walks of life including housewives and early retirees have been opting for this route. Many do their trading electronically — usually with personal computers [PCs] or telephones. Some market watchers attribute the increasing volatility of the financial markets in recent years to the high volumes these e-traders generate. In an age of greed, money has become a desirable commodity. It's the new status symbol — the standard, if you like — by which people's success or failure in life is being measured and compared.

Increasingly, we're seeing a two-tier world where a minority owns most of the wealth, while the majority hovers on the verge of poverty. According to the 1999 Forbes survey, the combined worth of the 400 richest Americans, totaling in excess of US$1,000 billion, was larger than the gross domestic product [GDP] of China. America's wealthiest person, Microsoft chief executive officer Bill Gates, whose net personal worth jumped to US$85 billion from US$59 billion in 1998, exceeded the Philippines' GDP of US$83.1 billion.

A recent study by the Center on Budget and Policy Priorities concluded that in spite of the current long-term U.S. bull market, income disparities between the richest and the poorest Americans have widened sharply during the past two decades and inequality may now be at its most extreme since the Second World War. The wealthiest 1% of households own 39% of the nation's wealth, compared with 13% of after-tax income. Even for a developing nation such as China, the income gap has been widening sharply. A recent study showed that 10% of its depositors hold 66% of the more than 6,000 billion yuan [US$720 billions] savings in banks.

Within these "first" and "third" worlds, there's also a two-tier society, where the rich tend to get ever richer and the poor, poorer still. The one thing they have in common is that there's no utopia. Both have problems although they may be facing very different ones. Third-world problems are mainly survival issues, — shelter, food, medical care, education and freedom of religious belief. First-world problems are mostly caused by excesses such as wealth, greed, envy, and materialism, which are replacing man's more basic need to fight for survival.

The first-world countries, however, are not immune to third-world problems. In fact, there is a growing core of people in even these wealthy countries that are living under third-world conditions. A recent study on hunger found that in spite of a decade of exceptional, unfettered prosperity in the United States, 3.5% of its population don't have enough to eat and 10% of families in 18 states and Washington D. C. its national capital, still go hungry daily.

As this gulf between the rich and the poor widens, there's a continuing erosion of the middle class – those who have annual incomes of about US$50,000 in the United States – and long considered the backbone of a democratic and capitalistic society. It's ironic that even as they are enjoying ever greater affluence and spending at an all time high, they have admitted, in recent surveys, to a growing sense of insecurity about their own financial future. They are making more money now than ever before – at least for the moment — but they must also work harder and longer hours just to cope. Prosperity, as many are beginning to discover, is no guarantee for a high quality of life. It seems the more they have, the more they want. This insatiable appetite for material goods and comforts, plus the constant specter that they may suddenly be laid off or be made redundant, has compounded their fear and uncertainty about their own long-term prospects.

An overview of globalization

These on-going major structural changes have profound implications on the welfare of people everywhere. The rapid advances in technology, innovations, globalization and deregulation in recent years have drastically changed how business is being done and operated. As worldwide global competition and deregulation escalates, there's a growing trend for companies from different continents to merge and consolidate their operations in order to achieve the economy of scale that is needed to survive. Just in the last year, an increasing number of multinational companies such as Daimler-Benz and Chrysler, Compaq Computer and Digital Equipment, Seagrams and Polygram, Exxon and Mobil, MCI WorldCom and Sprint, Glaxo Wellcome and SmithKline Beecham, Chase Manhattan Bank and JP Morgan & Co., PepsiCo and Quakers Oats have been taking this route.

A recent proposed merger between Mannesmann, a German industrial group, and Orange, a British mobile phone company, will illustrate just how complex and extensive these relationships can be. Orange, started in 1994, with about US$1.2 billion from Hong Kong conglomerate Hutchison Whampoa, was then capitalized at about US$28 billion. Hutchison, still Orange's largest holder, has agreed to vote its entire 44.5% holding in support of Mannesmann's friendly bid. When this deal is completed, Hutchison will then hold 10% of Mannesmann.

Even while this is happening in the fall of 1999, Mannesmann itself has become the target of a hostile takeover bid from Vodafone AirTouch, a British company, which became the world's largest mobile phone group after its US$62 billion purchase of AirTouch and merger with Bell Atlantic. Having established a leading position in the U.S. with these buyouts, Vodafone now looks to expanding in Europe, where Mannesmann is already its partner in key markets.

Pauline Tai

The final outcome was that Vodafone was successful in acquiring Mannesmann. But to appease regulatory competition concerns, Vodafone agreed in May 2000 to sell Orange to France Telecom for about US$46 billion (£31 billion or HK$360 billion), almost 57% more than the £19.8 billion Mannesmann paid when it negotiated to buy the company. The merged company, to be called New Orange, expects to have 30 million controlled subscribers by year-end.

As more such cross-border and/or cross-industry restructuring of companies takes hold, there are apt to be widespread, irreversible impacts on our global economies. These, in turn, will affect every aspect of our daily life.

The first mega-merger of the new millennium illustrates just how far-reaching these implications can be. When on 10 January 2000 America Online [AOL] announced its agreement to buy Time Warner for about US$184 billion, it was the world's largest such deal so far. AOL, the world's largest Internet service company and Time Warner, the world's largest media and entertainment company, will together create a media giant worth US$350 billion. To be renamed AOL Time Warner, the combined firm will control a wide cross section of products and services that range from CNN news and Time's stable of publications to Warner Bros. cartoons, films, music and other entertainment products to Internet service and data providers such as Netscape and CompuServe.

Barely two weeks later, Time Warner made an announcement of it's own. Time Warner and the EMI Group will merge the two companies' music units to create the world's biggest record company. Renamed Warner EMI Music, the new firm will be worth US$20 billion and have sales in excess of US$8 billion in some 70 countries. By buying EMI, Time Warner will get control of the last freestanding major music company, while EMI will get access to new Internet-based distribution channels for its music. Together they will have over 2,500 artists globally, release some 2,000 albums a year and have more than two million song copyrights.

Anxious to win regulatory approvals from the European Commission for its merger with AOL, Time Warner called off its plans for EMI Music in October 2000. With this out of the way, the Commission approved the AOL Time deal after the companies offered concessions to soothe competition worries. Across the Atlantic, the U.S. Federal Trade Commission [FTC] was also holding hearings on the proposed merger. After the two companies agreed to numerous pipeline-sharing arrangements with other independent Internet providers, the FTC finally gave its blessings on 14 December 2000.

The last hurdle was the U.S. Federal Communications Commission [FCC]. After long deliberations, the FCC gave its approval a year and a day after the companies announced their plans to merge. With headquarters in New York, they closed the deal on 12 January 2001. Its shares are now trading on the New York Stock Exchange under the symbol AOL.

4

Only time will tell how this mega-merger will pan out but a quick look at the numbers will show just how extensive their tentacles are going to be worldwide. AOL's 20 million customers will provide Time Warner with an audience for its television programs, movies, music and publications. Time Warner will open its fast cable-Internet lines to AOL, facilities that all the Internet service providers have been fighting to gain access. Some one billion people have access to CNN, 2.2 million to CompuServe and 35 million to HBO while Time Warner magazines have 120 million readers.

Is bigger really better?

For the companies and their shareholders involved, is bigger really better? Traditionally, approximately half of all mergers don't work out as planned. A look-back in history will show that these mega-deals often end up eventually as gigantic write-offs. General Electric [GE] bought investment banker Kidder Peabody in 1986 for US$600 million; GE tried to resuscitate Kidder by pouring in excess of another US$1 billion before selling it in 1994 for US$670 million. Dow Jones & Company, the publisher of *The Wall Street Journal* bought Telerate in the late 1980s for US$1.6 billion, spent millions more for restructuring and finally sold it in 1998 for US$510 million.

This doesn't mean there are no winners. Those who stand to benefit most from these marriages of convenience are the top managers or owners of these firms, the teams of investment bankers and lawyers who brokered and settled these deals.

For many of us, these mega-mergers will have serious implications on our own personal finance — as investors in these companies, as consumers of their products and services and, even more importantly, as employees in companies involved in such deals. As the global colossus created by these deals cover a wide cross-section of industries, their products and services will eventually touch on every facet of our daily lives.

Is bigger better for the common folks? The answer is probably a combination of yes, no and maybe, depending on which side of the equation you happen to be on at a particular point in your own life. Increasingly, you'll find yourself playing a variety of roles at the same time and often some of these may not be compatible with each other. For example, you held shares in the company you worked for through its pension plan. When the firm was taken over, your shares may have gone up but in the restructuring process, your job maybe downsized or simply eliminated.

In short, as the main twin purpose for these mergers is to cut costs and boost earnings, investors and possibly consumers in these companies should benefit — at least that's the proponents' rationale. For most workers in these companies, however, the outlook is less rosy. One easy way to reduce costs is to cut staff by offering tempting early-retirement packages to volunteers and closing down units that have duplications in the merged company. These changes signal the end of a long tradition where taking a job is considered a life commitment.   As globalization expands, many more workers – even for those who work in the public sector such as civil services — will have to face this new reality.

This on-going trend for companies to merge, consolidate, down size or restructure is causing a great deal of instability and irreversible changes in work places around the world.   In the industrialized countries, many manufacturing jobs have already moved overseas to locations where labor and land are cheaper. The "tiger" economies such as Hong Kong and Taiwan are also seeing a similar trend, where the more labor-intensive, low-skilled, low-tech jobs are moving across the border to mainland China.   Also contributing to the loss of jobs in this area is the recent economic crisis in Asia.   The longer this upheaval persists, the greater and more widespread its effects will be felt.

At the dawn of a new millennium, Asia is at a major crossroad that is quite similar to what the United States went through a decade or more ago.   The on-going structural changes that have been taking place in recent years in Asia are there to stay.   The sooner people there can accept this fact and start learning to adjust and live with these new realities, the better it will be for their own future.

How mega mergers may affect consumers

Although the current discussion on the mega-merger mania centers mainly on job security and financial concerns, there are other equally serious social and ethical implications.   Take the AOL Time Warner union.   On the surface, the synergy and the convenience that such a deal could engender sounds most inviting and enticing especially to those who enjoy having things neatly packaged for them.   But there's another side to this story as well.

With such a broad range of critical media products concentrated in one giant conglomerate, the fear is that, instead of exercising simple traditional cross-promotion and selling techniques, the combined firm may exert excessive control over what consumers are allowed to view, hear, read or download.   By dominating all sectors of the media markets, it could easily eliminate any competition from its rival firms.   Consumers may then be left to settle for less and at the same time be forced to pay higher prices for these AOL Time Warner products and services.

Even more troubling, however, is the possibility for conflicts of interest.   If the current trend continues, it will further erode the presses' already declining credibility.   The fine line between news and entertainment or promotion will be further blurred or eliminated completely.   For example, can any of the Time magazines write objectively and critically – or be allowed to do so — about the numerous firms or products that are controlled by the same parent company?

Instead of presenting different viewpoints, there may just be one corporate stand available. That's one of the possible pitfalls of cooperative ventures where companies in related industries cross promote and sell each other's products by sharing income that's been generated by their common customer base. In a world where newspapers, magazines, books, television news and even cartoons, CDs, videos and films are all part of the same corporate giant, one can't help but question the future state of journalistic integrity and impartiality.

Deregulation pros and cons

The recent economic crisis in Asia has also been giving an added impetus to advance and escalate world-wide deregulation, privatization and global competition in major industries such as banking, finance, telecommunications, utilities and transportation, including airlines and railroads. One area that has long-term impacts on consumers is the deregulation of financial services, which has become a top priority in the region following the 1997 economic crisis in Asia. For example, retirement savings schemes similar to the 401(K)s in the United States became available in Japan during 1999, and a mandatory retirement fund has been established in Hong Kong that became effective 2000.

As the United States was the first to deregulate these industries, what are the lessons learned from that experience? The idea for deregulation, at least theoretically speaking, is that it will lead to greater competition, generating more products at better prices for the consumers. In reality, however, it hasn't worked out quite that neatly. On a practical level, being inundated constantly with an increasing number of choices in banking products and pension schemes can make life for the consumer much more complicated and confusing.

For example, pre-deregulation, when accepting a job was a lifetime commitment, companies offered their employees just one pension plan. This scheme simply guaranteed them a certain set amount of income at retirement, as based on the number of years worked. The workers who quit before retirement age, however, were entitled to only the amount that they have contributed voluntarily. They must forfeit their pension rights to the portion the company contributed. In-house investment committees would manage these pension funds for their employees.

Post-deregulation, employees are offered a number of options, variations of the 401(K) — all cash accounts — which workers can take with them as they move from job to job. This flexibility, however, comes with a big price tag, especially for older workers approaching retirement age. Instead of guaranteeing a set retirement income and calculating that based on the years when the employee's wages were at their highest, the new system is geared more for the young, new recruits who, after a brief waiting period, will simply receive a certain amount, normally 5% to 10% of their annual salary, towards a cash pension account that they must now take charge of themselves. All the corporations would do today is to pick some investment fund managers who can offer a number of different investment products to their employees, who must then decide for themselves which of these options would suit their needs best.

In short, as consumers in such a deregulated environment, we are expected to take full responsibility for our own financial destiny. It is now up to us to acquire the information and knowledge that is necessary to arrive at the right decisions for ourselves. This is made more difficult as many of these "new" products being aggressively touted are often actually not really new but just a marketing ploy to increase sales. Maybe that's one reason why studies have shown that most employees who ended in the United States with 401 schemes often picked the easy way out by simply sticking it in a Federally-insured savings account at their local bank.

With interest rates at a record low in recent years, retirement funds invested in such savings accounts are barely rising on a par with inflation. At that rate, the fear is that when the time comes for these savers to retire, what they have invested won't be sufficient to generate the amount of income they'd need. This problem is exacerbated by the fact that a large number of "baby boomers" are expected to retire in the early years of the new century. This will create additional pressure on the social security system, as the number of workers needed to fund it will drop proportionately. As a result, many people may find they will have to continue to work long after retirement age just to make ends meet.

Are consumers getting a better deal?

As to whether the prices for these products have become cheaper or not, that's still open to debate. For most consumers, the real savings is probably minimal, if any, for financial institutions now add on fees even for services that were once either free or at very nominal amounts. In recent years, these service fees and other add-on charges have been increasing both steeply and rapidly.

When the U.S. banks deregulated back in 1986, many lower-income earners discovered they no longer could afford to have a checking account. The reason: to continue with "free" checking services which they enjoyed previously, they'd have to now meet certain minimums — these are usually set so high that most can't meet them. So instead, they'd be liable to a monthly fee, plus a charge for each check used. Some institutions even started charging a fee for opening or closing savings accounts — which ironically meant you're paying them to keep your money.

In recent years, similar fees have been cropping up and gaining popularity at financial institutions in other parts of the world where the sector has also been deregulated or is in the process of doing so. For example, to prepare for interest rate deregulation in July, two of Hong Kong's major banks recently announced a list of charges including a fee for using tellers to cash checks and a monthly fee on accounts below a certain minimum balance.

U.S. consumers are also getting mixed results from two other industries — airlines and electric utilities — that deregulated with great fanfare in recent years. So far, consumers have yet to enjoy any meaningful, long-term price breaks. What's certain, however, is that the quality of service today has deteriorated markedly. Air travelers are being plagued by constant delays and flight cancellations while consumers in California are suffering power blackouts and escalating electric bills. The two major electric utilities there are in such dire financial straits that they have requested urgent governmental assistance to help them stay in operation. A growing concern is that these power shortages may eventually spread to the rest of the country. As computer technology relies on electricity to function, if these blackouts continue unabated, the health of the global economy can be greatly affected.

With the U.S. economy on a roll for the last decade, there is a whole new generation of consumer-investors who have lived under this deregulated, overly competitive environment. If a bust should come as some experts are now predicting, how will they fare? A look at the other side of the world may give some inkling of what to expect. As certain areas in Asia such as Hong Kong have had good times from the 1980s to 1997, there are large segments of people who know only about up markets and nothing at all about how to cope in an economic trough. They have become complacent and have taken too much for granted. Unlike past down cycles, when things do eventually return to some form of normalcy — whatever that is — some of the recent structural changes are irreversible and destined to have long-term consequences in our daily lives, if what happened in the United States in recent years is any guide.

The down sizing that started there in the 1980s is still ongoing for some firms, even as the bull market charges on. Some companies are actually doing both staff cutting and hiring at the same time. This two-step process saves them money by weeding out the more experienced and costlier employees and replacing them with lower-priced, recent graduates. This creates a growing disparity between the earning power of the top-echelon directors and the work force. Also, as most of the workers made redundant were from the mid-management levels, many of these firms may, at some point in the near future, face a shortage of experienced managers needed to train and manage their new recruits. Instead of searching for another position, as they would have in previous times, many of those made redundant now would often decide to start their own businesses. Or they may simply give up and drop out of the work force entirely.

Privatization pros and cons

Another current buzzword is privatization, when cash-strapped governments sell off state-controlled companies such as airlines, railroads, utilities, postal and telephone services to raise funds. Even Hong Kong has caught the privatization bug as it sold in October 2000 one billion shares in the Mass Transit Railway Corporation [MTRC] for about US$1.1 billion [HK$9 billion]. Traditionally, for national security and other public policy reasons, industries that cater to public services were usually kept under state ownership. Today, proponents for privatization will tell you it's a win-win situation, as it will benefit both the company with greater competition and higher profits, and the consumer with better prices and services.

In practice, however, privatization has generally achieved rather mixed results, especially for the consumer. The reason: when large companies such as utilities and railroads are privatized, they in effect become beholden to their shareholders to provide a good return for their investments. Earnings then may take precedence over improving maintenance or other customer services. Britain, for example, privatized its railroads in the 1980s when Margaret Thatcher was prime minister. A string of rail accidents there recently prompted people to wonder if profit motives are compromising the quality of its service.

As can be expected, the largest number of state-owned enterprises was in places with planned economies such as the former Soviet Union. Through the 1980s, privatization was heavily promoted there as the solution to all their financial woes. Privatization, however, works only under certain conditions. Chances of success are often elusive.

China has also been trying hard to sort through their large number of outmoded state-owned enterprises. They're privatizing those with high potentials and closing down others that are considered unsalvageable. In the process, millions of workers are losing their jobs. It's still too soon to tell how things will work out there. But a great deal hinges on finding some successful solutions to this crucial livelihood issue, for the alternative could be massive social instability and political chaos.

Information versus knowledge

No matter where it's happening in the world, news such as market crashes, wars or natural disasters, are today being transmitted as they are occurring by a handful of major real-time wire services. We're being bombarded 24 hours a day with tons of information. Because we heard or saw it on TV, radio or the Internet, we assume we know what's going on in the world. But do we really?

News-gathering is a business like any other. The goal of these media firms is to make money. The competition between the major players such as Dow Jones and Reuters is intense. In their struggle to be the leader, they all strive for three goals: to be the first — translate that into being the fastest — with the most — that is, the largest quantity of information regardless whether it's of value or not — and the shortest — individual stories are cut to the bare bones. A little information can sometimes be more misleading than not having any at all, especially if what's given was wrong either in facts and/or interpretation. Although mistakes are usually corrected, most people tend to remember only the original version.

Most major news events, as covered in the popular press, are usually taken as isolated incidents. Rarely do we get enough relevant facts so we can form some clear picture of what implications or connections, if any, these events may have on our own lives. What compounds the problem is the tendency of lobbying groups to manipulate the press to their way of thinking. As the press tends to run as a pack and rely heavily on press releases, they often cover events in very similar ways.

In this era of double speak, style or image counts much more than substance or performance. Often, the packaging is more important than the content. The fine line between myth and fact can often be blurred or simply erased as the growing number of special interest groups vie for a shrinking pool of resources. Most public figures and organizations today hire image-makers to create enticing messages to sell their agenda or products.

The slogans these stage managers use are often either misnomers or in direct contradiction with their clients' actions. There's a tendency to look at the world through tinted shades and simplify everything into jazzy sound bites. So it's always good or bad, best or worst, black or white, all or nothing. In real life, of course, nothing can be so perfectly absolute. There are always innumerable shades of gray. No wonder then that even when we speak the same language, there can often still be an unbridgeable gulf between us.

To illustrate, let's take a quick tour of six issues — free press, free trade, democracy, capitalism, high technology and human rights — that show up almost daily in the world press.

Pauline Tai

These are issues the West — the U.S., in particular — has been pushing hard to promote to the developing world in recent years. Their advocates tend to talk only about what's good about them, but rarely, if ever, about their less positive aspects. As in any transactions, however, there are always tradeoffs for every positive has its negative side. In a way then, they concentrate mostly on what has worked for them – or what they think has, but rarely on whether it's appropriate, relevant, practical or achievable in places that don't have the necessary infrastructure, education and culture to support and nurture these ideals.

Free press

Sometimes even the titles such as "free" press and "free" trade is rather misleading, as when we look deeper into how things are actually done, we'll soon learn the word "free" is often used much too freely.

As a business, a "free" press can often be restrained not so much by political or social considerations but by purely economic reasons, simply because most media firms rely heavily on advertising dollars for their continuing financial health and growth.

Even the Internet is no longer as free as it was originally intended. A great deal of what it offers now is already being sponsored by advertisements. As the Internet expands into e-commerce and other activities, multinational corporations are already demanding stronger property rights such as copyright and royalties on music and other intellectual properties, as well as tough rules against computer frauds. Most Western governments have already passed Internet legislation that will address these concerns. For example, the United States enacted the No Electronic Theft Act of 1997 to fight and punish on-line crime.

Enacting such laws are the easy part. How to enforce them will be the bigger challenge as the Internet is a bit like a huge dam. Once its gates are opened, there's no stopping the rushing flow. Will our privacy be simply swept away as the ever-expanding traffic on this information superhighway takes over our lives?

Free trade

As for "free" trade, even among friends, there are numerous restrictions that are being applied to different industries and nations. Take, for example, the U.S. quota on textiles from China or its banana wars with the European Union.

Democracy

In its most popular format, democracy has in recent years been elevated to the status of a religion. For its devoted believers, any criticism against it is considered to be heresy. Like all forms of government, democracy comes in a variety of forms and degrees, depending on tradition, historical, social and economic developments. Freedom, however, doesn't come free. Like all things in life, there's always a price to pay.

Being members of a larger society, we're free only to the point where we don't infringe on the rights of others. The concomitant of democracy is responsibility. We're constantly being told about the wonders of freedom but rarely do we have a say in deciding how high a price we're willing to accept for having this privilege. Why give the whole story when half of it makes a better tale? This has become such a common practice today that many people are living in their own little world of half-truths.

Capitalism

As capitalism has developed in the United States, it has certainly benefited many people. But as it matures, it has also disenfranchised and displaced a great many others. We're witnessing an ever-growing divide between the rich and the poor — the north and the south, versus the east and west, as during the days of the cold war when the United States and the former Soviet Union vied for world supremacy. It's true that increasing prosperity can raise our standard of living and give us some sense of financial independence. At the same time, however, it can also lead to extreme materialism and greed. How heavy and costly a price all this will exact, only time will tell. Can a society survive over the long term, if its masses think only of grabbing as much of the material wealth as possible for themselves and not give a single thought to the common good?

High technology

No one can dispute, high technology has made some irreversible changes in the way we live and work. But in an increasingly multilevel and complex world, certain low tech products and services will also not only survive but will thrive in our new economy. We should always keep in mind that high technology is only a tool designed to make our life more productive and hopefully also more creative and cost effective. For computers to function properly, they still need the input of a human brain and the necessary infrastructure to support it.

A current question being asked in U.S. education circle is why after pouring billions of dollars of high technology equipments into their school systems in recent years, there's been negligible, if any, improvement in their students' achievement in either reading or mathematics. As many school systems around the world including Hong Kong are also currently in the process of updating and overhauling their curriculums, they should take advantage of the lessons learned in the United States so they can make better uses of their limited resources.

Hardware, like buildings, are just inanimate objects such as a container or a shelter used to hold, protect and organize a number of other items. They need skilled people and infrastructure to turn them into efficient, productive objects. But our leaders, no matter what their political slant, tend to take a rather myopic view of the world. They can readily understand tangible, visible assets such as buildings and hardware so they are willing to pour money into them. Most of them, however, lack the imagination needed to deal with the more abstract ideas and concepts that form the backbone of major policies that affect our daily life.

They also don't seem to realize or care that after the high-tech airports and the monumental complexes have been built, it's what go on in them and how these are operated, maintained and developed that really matter. To do a proper job, they'd need to have people with vision and ideas to run them efficiently and effectively. Talent and creativity don't happen in a void. They need constant nurturing and on-going education, training and opportunities.

With PCs, it's a fact young people are much more attuned to them than most grownups. But their interests are often quite different. While the adults' goal is to use PCs as a tool, some young people think of them as entertainment centers where they can play games, listen to music and watch films. There's nothing wrong with that, as long as it's also balanced with an academic component. Unfortunately, there are not enough technically knowledgeable grownups around to pass on to students what they should be learning.

According to a recent survey in the United States, only one in five teachers are able to use the PC proficiently. No wonder as the budget for hardware is almost 15 times larger than for teacher training — US$88 versus US$6. Parents are just as PC illiterate. For those willing to learn, it's often their children who will be teaching them rather than the other way round.

Although it's important to include training in technology in our schools, the current push to have PCs for students as young as possible is also troubling for a number of reasons. As is already well known in the United States, children of the TV age often have very serious problems concentrating. They are more susceptible to a variety of learning disabilities such as attention deficit disorder. Watching things on a monitor tend to promote skimming rather than spending time to learn to think and to concentrate on completing one task at a time.

A common problem is with reading and spelling. Even children who are able to pronounce and spell the words, they often have trouble understanding and relating to what the words really mean. Some would argue that with spell check in our PCs, why do you have to know how to spell? As the computer dictionary is based on common usage, when a word is used in a special context, you must still rely on your own knowledge to make the right choice.

A reminder of our recent experience with the calculator may help us to make better uses of the PC. Pre-calculator days, students had to learn the basic concepts of mathematics and the multiplication tables by heart before they were allowed to use an adding machine. When calculators became the norm, schools abandoned the old way. The problem, as we have since learned, was that people who rely solely on machines to do their arithmetic often ended up pretty much illiterate in mathematics.

In the real world, this can mean the loss of business as well, as witnessed at a recent event in a suburban town outside of Philadelphia, the City of Brotherly Love in the U.S. state of Pennsylvania. During one late morning last summer, a sudden heat wave increased the use of electricity to such a point that there was a complete blackout in the area. All the shops in the town's shopping mall closed their doors. When light came on, they reopened. Lunchtime shoppers started to reappear too, but within minutes, the lights went off again. At a local wine shop, a customer had picked some cases of wines and wanted to pay for them. The cashier replied that without electricity, he was not able to sell them. When asked why, he claimed he didn't know the prices, but when it was pointed out to him that these were all listed on the shelves, he replied irritatingly that he didn't know how to calculate what taxes to charge and that all customers must leave at once so he can re-lock the door until the electricity comes back on again.

There's a social and a health aspect to the technology issue as well. A major problem with being too computer-oriented is that the children will then be spending too much time with machines rather than with other people — a time when they should be learning how to establish and build interpersonal relationships. By working, studying and playing with others — both grownups and children — they learn to articulate ideas, communicate with others and work as a team. There's still no substitute for person-to-person exchanges where we can look each other straight in the eyes. These are all very basic social and communications skills that are best learned when we're young. These same skills are also critical to our own survival in the new economy, which will be increasingly knowledge based and service oriented.

Children today are leading an increasingly sedentary and isolated life by spending too many hours in front of a monitor — whether it's television or the PC, — and consuming too much greasy fast food and sweet caffeine sodas. This has great long-term implications on their health — both mentally and physically. Many are flabby and overweight with a weakened immune system. They are also more receptive to chronic diseases such as asthma, diabetes and hypertension. No wonder many suffer from mental and other learning disorders.

Grownups are facing an increasingly hostile work environment, as computer technology demand that they achieve ever-higher productivity. But when the systems crash or break down, production can be closed down completely. For workers this creates added tension, as they are usually not in control of the machines and must rely on technicians who are often located elsewhere. Life for the users of these systems can be extra frustrating and stressful. This state is often exacerbated by the fact that those who design and install the systems rarely understand the end users' needs and requirements. This lack of consultation and communication between the users and the technicians is unfortunately a common occurrence in the business world today.

There's probably an unhealthy trend for grownups as well. A recent Stanford University survey of Internet users found that some spend five hours or more each day on their PC. This meant an increasing number of people are now spending more time surfing the Net and less interacting or socializing with other human beings. Although the Internet offers a vast array of information, as well as opportunities to chat with complete strangers from around the world, this can never substitute completely for being with family or friends and having a meal together. The Internet can become a very lonely place if too much of one's life is spent there.

Human rights

Human rights mean different things to different people. So far there's no universally accepted definition. According to the United Nations, human rights include all the basic necessities of life such as shelter, food, medical care, education, the right to self-determination and the freedom of religious belief. The U.S. version, however, tends to concentrate more on democracy and personal freedom. No wonder then most human rights issues are a major source of misunderstanding and conflict between developing and developed countries.

As the top economic power in the world, it's natural the United States would want others to do its biddings. But it's just as true to say that other nations are following the leader blindly, assuming that if they'd follow its lead, they too can be as successful. Real life, however, is never quite that simple. What works over there often just doesn't work over here.

First, local traditions and past history must be taken into consideration. Second, to get anything to work requires some time in educating the general ·population, building the infrastructure and whatever other support systems that are needed to keep it going. More importantly, it must continuously be nurtured so it can expand and prosper unhindered.

Witness what's been taking place in the former Soviet Union with its quick attempts to convert to democracy and capitalism. Since the fall of communism nearly a decade ago, there's so far been only chaos and suffering for its masses. These things take time to be sorted out. After all, it took 200 years for the United States to come to this stage of development. In order for these two isms to flourish, it requires among other things, an educated, pluralistic society with a firm rule of law and a relatively free press.

If we were to manage well in this new economic environment, we'd have to develop a new mind set. Instead of just envying and copying other people's successes, we should learn from their experience and mistakes. No matter how good something may sound, the reality is that there are very few things, if any, that are truly portable and can be simply cloned and made to succeed just as well elsewhere. That's why it's vital that we know something of our own cultural heritage and traditions so we can develop a clear understanding of what will be effective and compatible with our own history and background.

Look, listen and learn

As we're being inundated with self-serving offers from all sides, it's healthy to be skeptical. Acquire the necessary knowledge so you can be confident and trust your own instincts. Don't accept things at face value. When in doubt, find out why. Look, listen and learn but don't be afraid to ask questions. Most knowledgeable people are more than happy to share their expertise. If you approach them with respect and civility, they will respond accordingly. If something sounds too good to be true, there's probably something fishy about it. Keeping yourself as fully informed as possible is the only way to protect your own interests. Then do your own analysis and see what makes the most sense for you. Learning to be observant, to think ahead and to be proactive rather than simply reactive to events will gain you better control of your own destiny.

Reality versus expectations

We live in a world of illusions where expectations are often taken as reality and reality as pure fiction or fantasy. A recent survey by the Hong Kong-based Breakthrough youth group found that most young people, aged between 12 and 16, believe soap operas are based on fact, with nearly half learning how to handle real-life problems from the characters. This poll also noted that these children spend an average of four hours a day watching television. This figure is quite similar to what's been recorded in the United States and elsewhere.

No wonder then that no matter how well prepared we are to face the "real" world, there will still be many surprises and possibly even a few traumas in store for us. The reality, whatever that is, if we deign to face it squarely, is often quite different from our perception or expectation. So it is with most things in life that we embark on for the first time. Take our first jobs. To start, most of us usually have very little idea of what we want to do, and even less of what we are really capable of doing. Yet our expectations are great although in reality, what we have to offer is usually minimal, at best.

Chances of falling into a "dream" job in your first try would be, indeed, a rare occurrence, especially during periods that are full of uncertainties and economic upheavals, when competition is at its most intense. For those with minimal education and little or no special skill or any practical experience under their belt, finding any job in this erratic economic environment can be a monumental task.

If you should find yourself in a position that you feel is beneath you, instead of feeling sorry for yourself, it is more constructive to figure out ways where you can somehow make the most of the opportunity at hand. Concentrate and take pride in doing a good job. Use your time and the available resources there to learn as much as you can about the company, the industry it's in, its competitors and the people who are involved in these businesses.

Still, being human, it's quite natural that at such times you may resent the idea of being stuck in something that seems of no interest to you. But the fact remains that sometimes such impositions can work to your advantage. By keeping an open mind, you will soon learn that this may be a blessing in disguise, as any work experience is better than none. In the long run, any accumulated experience will stand you in good stead, especially in today's work environment where cross disciplines are the growing trend. By trying new areas of endeavors, you may make some surprising discoveries. If nothing else, it will certainly open more doors for you in the future.

There's nothing wrong with having high expectations — in fact being ambitious and striving for a higher goal is always a healthy challenge — but it's also important to keep an eye on reality so you can get a better handle on what's practical and achievable at a certain point in your own personal development. Finding a balance between expectation and reality, of course, would be ideal, but in real life, that would be a rarity though not impossible. So it's still worthwhile to try as the more choices you have in life, the more opportunities you'll find coming your way. Why not make the most of them?

When times are good, you wish it would stay forever but the nature of things is that, nothing lasts forever. So enjoy yourself while it lasts even if it's something that you didn't expect. When times are bad, bearing this fact in mind can be a great consolation and a good reminder that it's best not to take things overly seriously as that too will soon pass. Having a sense of humor and the ability to laugh at yourself will definitely make life more pleasant and fulfilling all around.

The way we live and work

Today's work place already expects and demands a great deal more of its workers than ever before. This is also changing how we live and deal with each other. Chances are such demands will increase at an accelerating pace as technology, innovations, deregulation, privatization and globalization continue to advance and intrude into every facet of our lives. In this new world, education will play an increasingly critical role. Until quite recently, a high school diploma may have been all you'd need to earn a good living. Today, you may need not just one university degree, but possibly two or three, just to get your foot in the door. Increasingly with technical positions such as servicing on-line customer queries, a college degree is required just to answer those calls.

This shift in market requirements has eroded the wages for high school graduates. The income gap between college and high school graduates has never been wider. The former earns 60% to 70% more today than the latter, compared with only 30% just a few years back. From what can be culled from recent events, this gap will continue to widen and, as with everything else, at an increasingly faster pace than ever before. To cope in this highly competitive environment, workers with only high school educations must be willing and able to learn new skills and adapt themselves to the evolving business climate.

Formal education, however, is only just one of the numerous tangible pre-requisites that employers may demand from job applicants. Other intangible traits they will look at include your own personal interests, outlook and, most importantly, your attitude, as well as your character, temperament and background. When faced with candidates who share similar education and experience, employers will often give more weight to someone with the personal traits they feel will be most compatible with their corporate culture and business.

In this evolving and often erratic economic environment, unless you take the time to find out what the overall changing requirements are and then prepare yourself accordingly, you will likely encounter many roadblocks later on. You must make it a top priority to learn to take charge of your own life and be responsible for your own and your family's on-going well being.

People who will fare well in this fast changing and competitive milieu will share some common basic skills and attitudes. These will be explored in detail in Chapter 3.

The age of multi-choices — "multilism"

In simpler times before industrialization advanced to high technology, life ran on a monorail in agrarian societies. Because choices, if any, were limited, life at that time may seem to us today less complicated and confusing. In fact, however, everyday life on the farms no matter where in the world was so hard that to survive everyone, including young children, would toil from dawn to dusk. Having lots of children was one way to grow your own labor force and to insure against early death due to sickness, poverty and other natural disasters. Despite the hardships and the lack of material comforts, life was less stressful. People were endowed with certain intangible assets such as a firm conviction of self-identity, common sense and community, which instilled in them a stronger sense of belonging.

A quick look back

In a way, the teen evolution in recent U.S. history is reflective of what's been happening worldwide. A quick look at this phenomenon will give some better perspective on how drastically things have changed in just this century and what implications these changes may have on our own life in the coming decades.

Until the 1920s, only about a quarter of the high-school-age youth in the United States attended school. The vast majority of adolescents worked on farms. Then came the Great Depression of the 1930s, when most of them were thrown out of work. To keep them off the streets, they were sent to school instead. This trend to extend the age of innocence was interrupted in the 1940s by the Second World War and in the 1950s by the Korean War. Young men who fought in these wars were given financial incentives on their return to continue their education. This brought more mature students into the American schools and universities; and started yet another new trend, one that is still continuing and thriving today.

During the prosperous 1950s the image of youth began to evolve into that of the rebel and started the rock-and-roll boom. Business saw the great potential of this untapped market. The baby boomers of the 1960s were high on self and low on conformity. The Vietnam War added fuel to their battles and resulted in great turbulence around the world. The two oil crises in the 1970s and early 1980s plunged the United States and its Western allies into conflict with the Organization of Petroleum Exporting Countries [OPEC]. High inflation and interest rates during this period caused such economic havoc that many companies had to resort to drastic measures in order to survive. This started the restructuring process that's still on going in the United States, despite a roaring bull market in the past decade.

It's hard to imagine that until the 1940s, most people lived in smaller communities, where their families may have been settled for some generations and may have even worked for the same firm. Children often followed in their parents' footsteps. Accepting a job was a lifetime commitment. Banks offered only a single passbook savings account; insurance companies sold just one type of life policy and, in most areas, there was just one single telephone company and an electric utility.

A quick look forward

Today, an Internet-connected world seems to have run amok, jogging along nonstop at breakneck speed on multi-tracks extended in all different directions at the same time. From consumer goods, to investment products to religious or political convictions, there are options and choices galore. Is faster and more really better? In fact, there's so much out there already that for most of us, we'll never be able to sort them all out — never mind about taking full advantage of them. Take the PC. Most come today loaded with such a great variety of software programs that few people can ever really make full use of them all.

As a matter of fact, both nations and individuals have been slow to grasp the implications of "multilism." After all, so far most people have been educated to function with a one-track mind rather than accepting and planning ahead on multilevels. Our human brain seems to need time to process and make sense of these changes and at any one time, it can only cope and retain a certain amount of information. Nevertheless, market activities are occurring worldwide at all levels of society on both tiers, making even more options and choices available.

For example, even as globalization takes hold, there are parallel channels towards building more regional blocks. The United States, Canada and Mexico has the North America Free Trade Agreement [NAFTA]; the 15 European countries including Germany, France, Italy and the United Kingdom have the European Union [EU]; and the ten southeast Asian countries including Brunei, Indonesia, Singapore and Thailand, have the Association of Southeast Asian Nations [ASEAN].

Since the 1997 financial crisis, the ASEAN group has been considering the establishment of a broader East Asian regional economic bloc that will also include Japan, China and South Korea. According to Fred Bergsten, director of the Washington-based Institute for International Economics, "the aggregate economy and external trade of East Asia is about as large as those of the United States and European Union. The region's collective purchasing power – US$9.4 trillion in 1997 – surpassed the EU and the US."

At the dawn of a new century, the spread of "multilism" may see a different lineup of major economic forces. Since the Second World War, the three largest economies have been the United States, Japan and Germany. With the arrival of 1999, monetary union became a reality as planned, as 11 of the 15 EU members qualified for participation in this historical event. With the euro as its common currency, Europe would now be in a much better position to compete with the United States — that, at least, is its proponents' hope. The EU now has a combined population of approximately 370 million, compared with 280 million for the United States, and a gross domestic product [GDP] of US$8,458.3 billion versus US$9,190.4 billion respectively.

In the coming years, there will be a major shift in the lineup of the largest economies. The EU will compete head-on with the United States for second place as China looms to be the largest economy by 2020, resuming the number one spot that it held in 1820, according to a recent Organization for Economic Cooperation and Development [OECD] report.

Even as the major nations get ever more powerful, there will also be an increase in the number of tiny nation states, as the remaining dependent territories strive to achieve self determination. Witness how the United Nations membership has changed through the years. At its inaugural meeting in San Francisco following the Second World War in 1945, there were 51 members. By 2000, there are 188 members in the United Nations.

Instead of big world wars, there will continue to be many more little wars such as what we have witnessed in Iraq, Afghanistan, Kosovo, East Timor and Africa in recent years. Large segments of the local population will be completely displaced and economies that were already on the edge would become even worst off than before. Foreign peace-keepers, often thrown under the UN umbrella after the fact, will take over as the police force or the protective government for an undetermined period of time.

It's difficult to determine what, if anything, constructive has been achieved through these little wars. What's certain is that the basic problems they were supposed to solve remained intact and perhaps, they even added a few new ones including the destruction of most major infrastructures and priceless ancient monuments. To rebuild from scratch only what's needed just to survive would require huge sums of money — amounts these countries naturally didn't have. So they have to rely on outside assistance. Such financial resources including borrowings would become increasingly scarce as an increasing number of ruined nations with little future prospects sought financial help to rebuild.

The UN itself has also been under a great deal of financial stress in recent years, as the United States, until recently its largest contributor and debtor, refused to pay back the more than $1 billion it still owes. Most people blame the UN for its lack of leadership even though they know little, if anything, about the organization or its many activities around the world. As a club of nations, the UN has no power or army of its own, except what the members decide to confer upon it. They decide what the UN can and cannot do. The UN cannot even enter a country unless it's been invited to do so.

If individual countries have problems getting a consensus, you can imagine what it would be like to have 188 nations trying to agree on taking action on anything cooperatively. The UN deserves our support. It's a place where leaders of differing political persuasions can meet with each other in relative calm.

There's another side to the UN that we don't hear so much about that has made great contributions in social, economic and technical assistance to the developing countries. Sister organizations such as the United Nations Children's Fund [UNICEF], World Health Organization [WHO] and the United Nations High Commission for Refugees [UNHCR] have been at the forefront of helping those most in need around the world.

Whether it is governments, companies or schools, being the largest in size can often be more of a burden than a benefit as it can mean being tied down with too much red tape. In fact, recent developments have shown that at a certain size, such entities tend to become unmanageable and harmful to its constituents. A recent survey of U.S. schools found that of all the students involved in armed assaults, 71% attended schools with 1,000 or more students. Large schools, like any over-sized organizations, can be overwhelming and forbidding. They are easy places to get lost in and can cause exacerbated violence and loneliness.

We often forget that the success of any organization or nation depends on the people who work, study and live there. Human beings are by nature social creatures. For them to attain a certain quality of life they must have a firm identity and a strong sense of community. Most people are adverse to changes. That's why all new inventions take time to develop a following and be assimilated into the public conscience. People need time to learn and adjust their thinking to accept these major changes. Inventions such as electricity, the automobile, the telephone and the airplane took an average of 50 or more years to become a readily acceptable and affordable mass product. During this period, new products tend to follow a life cycle of its' own.

The latest such revolution involves the combination of two major industries – that of information and technology. As with the initial stages of any new inventions, market psychology plays a more crucial role than profits. Those who now speculate feverishly on the Internet-related companies should take a step back and look at what actually happened to some former star inventions such as the automobile and the airplane. At its heyday, there were hundreds of carmakers in the United States. Today there are just three, including one, Chrysler that was recently bought by Daimler-Benz, the German firm that makes the Mercedes. The merged company is now known as Daimler-Chrysler. Of the thousands of airlines that once existed, only a handful of major ones are still flying. In recent years, a good number have gone bankrupt, including the U.S.'s flagship Pan American or more commonly known as PanAm.

As the multinational companies merge with each other to become ever-larger entities, we're also seeing an increasing number of entrepreneurial startups sprouting out of everywhere. The Internet is changing how business is being conducted. A virtual factory requires little start-up capital. It needs no particular fixed assets or physical inventory, for that matter. Anyone with an idea and a PC may set up shop and if the idea takes off, that founder can be a multimillionaire in no time at all. For many others, however, success can be rather illusory and losses a constant companion.

How the increasing number of new-economy companies are financing their growth is also changing the financial markets. Instead of borrowing from banks or offering bonds to the public, as most traditional companies would often do, these newcomers would rather issue equity so investors can share in both their good and bad fortunes. Instead of paying high salaries to their staff, they give them stock options. As more e-firms go this route, it's inevitable the financial markets will react quite differently than previously, possibly upsetting many of the traditional economic theories, rules or practices. During this period of transition, there will be a great deal of uncertainty and turmoil. However, for the adventurous, there will be many challenging and possibly even profitable opportunities as well.

Nevertheless, through all these on-going changes, there are some positive and irreversible developments. As a majority of these new startups provide services that cater to the retail sectors, consumers are finally getting the breaks that were previously available only to corporations or large investors. Unlike previous times, when you have to rely on middlemen such as stockbrokers, travel or real estate agents to handle your transactions, now you can go directly to the source. You may even get a price break for handling the deal yourself.

To be successful in this environment, companies must be adept at combining both high and low-tech capabilities in their daily operations. While computers handle most of the back-office chores such as record keeping, the servicing of customers is still very much a human encounter, granted the communication itself is done mostly electronically. This means people who work in these companies must be well versed on how to work the PCs, deal with customer inquiries and orders promptly and accurately. To handle these issues properly, they must also know their inventory well. Quality service then is key to these hi-tech firms' success.

Corporations that used to rely on keeping their consumers ignorant as a way to enhance their profits can no longer get away with such unfair practices. Critical information and other data that were previously available only to their largest customers are now there on-line, often for free, to anyone who is interested. As a result, in recent years individual consumers have become increasingly better educated about the market place and they have now the capability to shop in the comfort of their homes for the best values. No wonder then traffic on the Net is doubling every 100 days.

Governments too must learn to be more in tune with its own citizenry. With more developing countries adopting some form of free-market economy, the hope is that their population-at-large would become better educated and achieve a certain level of financial independence. With some economic stability, greater personal freedom will follow as they assume more responsibility for their own destiny. Maybe then they'll start carrying their own weight; identifying more solidly with their community and being more involved with achieving some goals aimed at the common good.

What you're getting a glimpse of today is the basis of the new economy. Along with speed, volume and variety, it is also borderless, flexible, expanding and innovative. Along with the growing options, there will be many more opportunities available. These constant changes will bring ever more unlimited choices and new, untested challenges, as well as extreme volatilities, growing risks and constant uncertainties and changes.

For the creative and adventurous, this is an exciting and challenging arena to be playing in. People who will fare well in this environment will tend to be multicultural and multilingual; they will think multidimensionality, multi-directionally, multiethnically, multifacetedly, multifariously, multifunctionally, multi-gradedly and multilaterally; and build multi-channel, multicolor, multimedia multinational corporations. With a bit of luck, they may even be the new multimillionaires — or possibly even multibillionaires — of the new millennium. But unlike previous decades, when most of these nouveaux riches were born and bred in the United States, we'll be seeing many more of them coming from other continents. Don't be surprised if a good number of them will be from Asia and possibly from some other places that have yet to be added to the roster of world-press coverage.

As a growing number of people become enlightened and assimilated into this new, multilevel economic environment, it is hoped that we'll see more caring societies emerge from a shrunken and more interdependent world. As a result, the quality of life for the majority will also improve immeasurably. Who knows, as the future leaders of this wondrous world, with some thoughtful planning and hard work, you too can play an active and invaluable role in making this a reality.

2. Know Yourself

Different seasons, different needs

In life's changing seasons, you will be faced with innumerable challenges as well as different needs to fulfill and new goals to meet. We may be individuals with our own free will. But as human beings sharing the same universe, we all go through the same life cycles. At different seasons, we are called upon to play different roles. Sometimes we even get to repeat the same roles but at another season. Let's start with the master script from the beginning.

Spring

This is the season when all things in nature burst forth with new life. First, the leaves, and with the proper care, then buds will appear, which eventually will turn into lovely blooms. So it is with our own life. An infant with loving nurturing will grow into a healthy child and later on into a creative, productive young adult. In an ideal world, childhood should be a carefree, happy period. Unfortunately, in our industrialized, high-tech world, we are increasingly forcing our children to be grownups before their time.

Summer

Summer is when life is in full bloom and young adults complete their education and enter the real world of work. For many, it is a time to start building on their profession, earning some money, falling in love, getting married and having children. It is also a time to start accumulating assets, setting some aside for a rainy day and planning for the future.

Autumn

When leaves turn to red and gold before falling off completely, it is autumn. For matured adults, this is a time for winding down — the children should now be primarily on their own — so it is a time to think and do more for ourselves again. But this is getting to be easier said than done, since our world is changing at such a rapid pace that most conventional norms are no longer applicable today. Children are now staying home longer and spending more years studying than ever before. At the same time, our aging parents may need our help financially, physically and/or emotionally. At some point during this cycle, we should also start preparing — or at least start thinking about — the practical aspects of our own retirement.

Winter

Ideally, this is a time to hibernate, to rejuvenate, and to do what we have always wanted to, but never had the time or the resources to do so. It is a time to enjoy and to share the good things in life with family and friends. With some thoughtful consideration and planning, it is possible to make this a reality.

The in-between season

Real life, however, is usually not as straight forward as nature's script. In post-industrialized economies such as the United States and Europe, the family is going through some drastic structural changes. These same changes can also be seen in Hong Kong and China. Along with more options and opportunities, both men and women are also called upon to play more roles — roles that are often no longer very well defined and they may even contradict with each other.

For example, as an increasing number of women join the work force, there will be many more two-income families. Women are already having children later — if they have any at all. With one in three or four marriages ending in divorce, there will be many more second families. The advancement in medical technology and care means better health and a longer life expectancy for most people. But living longer doesn't guarantee a high quality of life.

With the graying of America, Europe and selected areas in Asia, there are fewer young workers to provide sufficient funding for social security or other welfare programs. For many, the only solution is to work longer or to start a second career. All this adds up to a muddying of life's seasons, and the in-between seasons will play an increasingly larger role in our lives.

Pauline Tai

Some of us may take longer to get from one stage to the next, or we may even have the seasons reversed. Some may repeat seasons, or skip one altogether. It's ironic that just as our younger children are increasingly being forced to be grownups before their time, their older siblings are opting to stay longer in schools – often also staying at home with the parents — and delaying their entry into the workforce.

Most of us go through life without giving the seasons much thought. We expect things to simply happen at the appropriate time. As more choices and options become available, it may be necessary to give the seasons some thoughtful consideration, especially if you want to make the most of them. Otherwise, there is always the possibility that, if we are not careful, we may end up being in- between seasons all our lives.

Most major decisions we have to face in this adventure through the circle of life demand that we must first truly get to know ourselves — what it is that we really want. By having a firm grasp and understanding of our own strengths and weaknesses, we will have a better chance of making the correct decisions on critical issues such as education, career and personal finance — the three areas that have life-long effects on our own and our family's well-being.

Take, for example, investment decisions. Before we can decide whether to put our money in stocks or bonds or mutual funds, we must first find out who we are, how comfortable we are with risk, and what we want to accomplish. The same can be said for education and career. If we know what we would like to do, we could better prepare ourselves and seek out ways to achieve those goals.

Which face is the "real" you?

Have you ever wondered how very complex and so full of contradictions we human beings really are? Who are we? What makes us tick? It's quite true that no two of us are ever alike, but on the other hand, we're also being told that we're born equal with our own free will so we can decide for ourselves what we want to do with our own lives.

Life is, of course, full of contradictions and not so very simple. To know and understand yourself, you must first take a thoughtful look at our common past. Nature, which endows human beings with basically two critical components, retains control of the key source of our essential being. Whether we're born in a rich or poor country, have good or bad parents – these are issues that we have absolutely no choice but to accept, and if possible, to make the best of what we've been given.

The one area where we can make our own imprint is what we're able to develop and acquire through exposure, education and experience. For us to fare well in our own efforts, we must first, however, know something about our own origin and history, as the two are irrevocably intertwined. Who we are and where we come from will play key roles in how we'll develop and behave in life. In short, our background can play a positive or a negative role in our future growth. It's up to us entirely how we want this balance to tip. But if we're like most people, we'll often be our own worst enemy by creating problems or setting roadblocks that would hold us back from leading a happy and constructive life.

Within this dual framework, each of us really leads two lives – an exterior and an interior life. What the world sees of us is our outer face – mostly the physical trappings that money can buy. Our heroes today are the celebrities who lead the fast life making the quick bucks. We envy them not so much for their brains or talents as for all the things that they can physically possess. We see or hear only about their public image, but we have no idea of the personal price that they must pay to get there or what they really feel about their own lives.

If we were to function as healthy whole beings, we must try to keep a balance between our emotional, spiritual, intellectual and physical lives. The face we show to the exterior world should complement and be compatible with the one that we must face internally. Unfortunately, an increasing number of us today are so preoccupied with creating a good image with our external faces that we have completely neglected and lost touch with our other inner self.

Outward beauty such as a gorgeous face without character or soul is, after all, just an empty shell. With plastic surgery so common these days, most people who can afford the price can now pay to get the face they deem is pretty. So looking at just the exterior cover, whether it's your own or others, can give only a very superficial and often misleading view.

Eight questions to help you get in touch with yourself

Getting a firmer handle on your own character will pinpoint and clarify your own strengths and weaknesses. Having a clear picture of what these are will help you develop ways to improve yourself and to turn the negative aspects into positive ones. Knowing your own weaknesses will help you to find ways to overcome them or possibly to even make use of them to your advantage. Here are eight questions to help you get started getting to know yourself better.

	Questions	**Notes**
1.	*What temperament or personality type are you? Are you a people's person or a loner?* If you're a loner, you will probably prefer work that you can do alone such as research and not having to deal with the public. You may play sports such as jogging or tennis rather than soccer or football. *Are you calm and generally laid-back or are you nervous and high-strung? Are you shy or out-going? Are you timid or arrogant?* Knowing your own stress threshold will help you avoid many unpleasant and often unnecessary situations. For example, some people can get things accomplished only under strict deadlines while others find such restrictions nerve wracking and nonproductive. If you can't handle deadlines, then jobs such as a news reporter or a stock exchange floor broker are not for you. *Are you a leader or a follower? Are you a doer or a dreamer? Are you an ideas person or an implementer? Or both? Are you artistically or scientifically inclined?* Leaders and followers have quite different temperaments and thus behave and act differently as well. Having some ideas of your own leanings and capabilities will give you an instant roadmap to what route you should follow in your search for courses to take or careers to pursue and develop.	

Questions	Notes
Do you consider yourself a mono-cultural or multicultural person? If the latter, you'll want to be in the forefront of world economic development instead of just participating at the local or regional levels. If globalization were to take off, as it's been predicted it will, local and regional markets are destined to shrink further unless they can find new ways to justify themselves. You'll want to study languages and other subjects that would give you a broad view of the world.	
2. ***Are you adventurous and do you like to take chances? Or are you the exact opposite and tend to dislike changes and uncertainties? How much risk do you like?*** Some of us thrive on risk, while others abhor the slightest bit. As everything we do in life involves some degree of risk, it would be to our advantage to work out a certain level that we could accept comfortably. Knowing your own risk threshold will enable you to search for the areas of studies, jobs and investments that will suit your own risk level and temperament.	
3. ***What do you perceive to be your strong points? What are your weak points?*** Are you, for example, a procrastinator or a no-nonsense activist? Are you industrious or are you lazy? Are you dependable and trustworthy or are you unreliable and untrustworthy?	

Questions	**Notes**
Do you need constant supervision or can you be relied upon to take whatever initiatives are necessary to get something done? If you have a problem, will you spend time to solve it or will you simply give up when the going is tough? Are you decisive or wishy-washy? If you've made a mistake, would you have the courage to admit it? Are you a good team player or a prima donna? Are you secretive and unhelpful? Or are you open, friendly and helpful? Are you generous or miserly – not just with your money or other possessions but also with your time and knowledge?	
4. *What lifestyle suits you?* Are you a city person? Or, do you prefer the countryside? Where you live will depend, to a large extent, on your temperament and will definitely have a long-lasting effect on how and where you work, live and spend your money.	

Questions	Notes
5. ***Do you have dreams?*** As objectives and goals often begin as dreams we should never just discount them. They can often provide sound ideas that can be developed into actual plans for action. ***What are your objectives?*** ***Do you have any goals?*** Nothing gets done unless you have a plan. So it is with studying, working and investing. Generally, it is good for the morale to have some objectives that are short term so you can see some results relatively soon; and then some longer-term ones as a means of planning for the future. When setting your objectives, think objectively and be realistic about your priorities. It's always a good idea to set a deadline for their completion. For example, if you are a high school student, your immediate goal is to get good enough grades so you will be able to attend a university of your choice later on. If you're just starting out in a new career, one of your first financial goals is to save an emergency fund. After that, it is time to accumulate assets so one day you can begin investing seriously.	
6. ***What's power and money mean to you? What does success mean to you?*** Having tons of money? Or being able to excel	

Questions	Notes
doing something that gives you pleasure and satisfaction? What attracts you more: a higher salary or an interesting job that has good learning potential and future prospects?	
7. ***Is image important to you? Why?*** Is image more important to you than performance? Are you more concerned with how others look at you than what you think of yourself?	
8. ***Are you easily intimidated and/or impressed by other people's power and money?*** If so, just put yourself in their place for a change. If you have those millions and live in those mansions, just imagine the burden these perks can impose on you – not to mention the responsibilities.	

3. Help Yourself

Taking the first steps

Once you have gotten in touch with your true self, it is time to consider what steps you can take to help you achieve your goals. In this age of the Internet, where information of all types is readily available either free or at nominal prices, there is absolutely no excuse for anyone to claim ignorance.

Following are two sets of ideas to get you started. The first takes a critical look at what basic skills and attitudes are needed to cope in this new economic environment. The second describes briefly some economic basics that will help you develop a better understanding of what's happening in the world around you.

People who would fare well in the fast-evolving milieu of the new economy will share some common basic skills and attitudes such as the following eight:

A self-identity

You have a certain confidence and knowledge of your own aspirations, as well as the commitment, courage, determination, discipline, focus and motivation to take control of situations in order to realize them. In short, you have a good head on your shoulders and can think for yourself. You are proud of your strong points but are just as aware of your weaknesses and limitations. Getting the two to complement each other will create new opportunities for you to explore. You have some idea of what you want out of life; you know what you enjoy doing and how to seek out the opportunities to achieve those goals.

Leading a healthy, harmonious life is the key to achieving these goals. Like any piece of great machinery, our body requires constant care to keep it in perfect working condition. If you acquire sound habits early on, it's really quite easy to lead a healthy lifestyle. All you need is a certain amount of discipline so you can follow a balanced diet, get sufficient sleep and do regular exercises. By achieving good health, you'll be in much better condition to face the many challenges that you'll encounter as you journey through life.

Professionalism

If you expect others to treat you as a "pro," you must first act like one. It's crucial to develop good work habits such as being on time, meeting deadlines, playing and carrying your own weight in a team, exercising good communications skills, accepting constructive criticism graciously and being willing to speak out, when the occasion calls for it. Being observant and considerate, keeping an open mind and listening to others are also important. If nothing else, you may learn something new.

There's a common misconception that professionalism applies only at work. But in fact, the word only encompasses all the necessary traits that all people in civilized societies should have learned while growing up. These are habits that would stand you in good stead in whatever you'll do in life. On top of the list would be to develop a strong sense of common decency and integrity. That means you can be trusted in everything you do from keeping to yourself information that's confidential, to following up with things that you promise to do, to telling the truth, to admitting an error when you've made one.

A recent survey in the United States found that widespread cheating has become an accepted practice in all levels of education from secondary schools to universities. When asked, students claimed they do it because everyone else does it. Being a common practice certainly doesn't make it right. By cheating, these students are in effect hurting themselves.

The only way to get ahead is to learn to think for yourself and trust your own convictions. If you feel something strongly and can support it with the proper facts and figures, by all means, go for it. After all, if everyone is too afraid to be different, then nothing new will ever be discovered in the world. But keep in mind that how you present your ideas is just as important as the content. So organize accordingly and be prepared for a constructive and collegial discussion, where any disagreements will be treated with mutual appreciation and respect.

With growing demands on your time, it's often helpful to make a conscious separation between your work and personal life. Chances are you'll be caught up in juggling a variety of different roles. Increasingly often these may create conflicts of interest for you. To ensure you keep your own integrity intact, as you move from job to job at growing frequencies, you must stay vigilant of this fact.

Keeping your work and private lives separate can also help to clarify some of the many contradictions in life that we must face daily. Often these issues involve core ethical values that deal with what's right or wrong. What's more confusing is that sometimes an issue can be both depending on which criteria you base them on. For example, under our judicial system, guilt is based whether a crime can be proved to have occurred. But certain religions will also consider unacceptable thoughts such as lusting for your neighbor's spouse with as much weight as if adultery has been committed. Or, why is it acceptable for people who work as soldiers or police officers to kill while on their jobs but if they were to do so as civilians, it'd be considered a crime?

Where possible avoid dragging personal problems to school or to the office and vice versa. Be considerate and attentive to your classmates or colleagues as you would with your family and friends. A smile and a helping hand can do wonders for how you treat others is often how they will treat you in return. Even in the most competitive environment, there's room for civility and for sharing knowledge with each other. This is especially important where teamwork is increasingly the norm. A high degree of collaboration and cooperation is necessary in most work places today. If you respect others, chances are they'll respect you in return as well.

Another danger in modern day life is that your studies or job can be so all-consuming that they take over your whole life. At day's end, what is important is not the job but the people, starting with your family, friends and colleagues.

Flexibility

Things are changing so very rapidly that it is impossible for anyone to know everything so it is important to stay as flexible as possible and to keep an open mind. But this doesn't preclude you from holding true to your own values and opinions. You just have to go some steps further and be more proactive and adaptive. Being prepared makes it easier to face the inevitable changes that are sure to loom in your future. It pays to take charge of your own life rather than simply waiting for things to happen.

Having a firm foundation in time management will also help you cope and be flexible when necessary. Knowing how you apportion the hours of your days is a bit like having a budget for your finances. A time manager will ensure that you didn't omit anything that should have your attention during any 24-hour day.

After deducting the hours needed for daily necessities such as sleeping, eating, going to school and doing homework and/or working, you must still find time to relax and socialize with family and friends, as well as to be alone by yourself. That's why if you spend an inordinate number of hours watching TV or surfing the Net, you'd be losing out on a good part of your life.

In the current fast-evolving economic climate, the job you have today may not be here tomorrow. The one consolation is that these changes will also bring many new opportunities — most of which probably never existed before. The more adventurous — especially those gifted generalists who have also cultivated expertise in critical niche areas — may even be able to take full advantage of these developments and create their own positions by combining a number of these new opportunities and disciplines.

So it's important to develop an ability to focus, adjust and to take control, when the circumstances arise or change. This includes, assuming the situation is the right one for you at that point in time, a willingness to go wherever the job is and work whatever hours or shifts that are required. The nine-to-five type of jobs are fast becoming obsolete, as more and more businesses go global by being opened 24 hours a day. Some companies, so far mainly in northern Europe and the United States, have also been experimenting with flexible-time schedules, where workers rotate on different timetables, depending on seasonal workloads and/or personal preferences. Another growing trend: an increasing number of people are working from home, which blurs further the distinction between working and leisure hours.

When considering a change in jobs, you should look at not just the salary but also what additional potential the new situation may have to offer you. Will you get more responsibilities? More chances to grow and learn new things? More importantly, will it lead you one step nearer your ultimate goal? At a certain point, the quality of life may also be an issue. What's the point of making tons of money if you don't have time to enjoy it with your family and friends? Many are now coming to that realization and would rather take a lower-paying job than working and traveling nonstop in a job that gives little personal satisfaction.

Be positive

Negativism kills — that's a known fact. Many people fail in their endeavors because they have such a low esteem of themselves and their abilities. Most people who have a positive and realistic attitude also tend to have a better sense of humor and view the world and themselves with a healthy dose of skepticism.

Developing a positive attitude towards life and having some confidence in yourself will help you not only to cope with the fluxion around you but also to be more adventurous and try new things, when they come your way. Many people lose out because they refuse to take any chances. They're afraid of changes and the risks that are associated with them. Ironically, life is full of changes, uncertainties and risks. Often you may have no choice but to face them squarely or be enveloped and stifled by them. Getting a firm handle of your own risk and stress thresholds will help you to make sounder and more educated decisions on the major issues in your life.

As the fear of change is mostly due to ignorance, gaining some knowledge about what's at hand can help you to understand the situation better and may in turn give you some confidence in yourself. Being more confident means you'll be able to exert more control in your own affairs and can take the appropriate steps to do whatever is necessary to move forward.

You can also help yourself by identifying priorities and concentrating on your immediate goals. Complaining and procrastinating only wastes time. You might as well spend this time doing something creative. Setting priorities with deadlines and concentrating on them will soon bring you some real results.

Learning to make the most of your time and available resources will also help. Instead of dilly-dallying when you are called upon to do something you do not like, it would be much more constructive to take advantage of the opportunity by learning as much as you can about the matter at hand. By being open minded, you might make some surprising discoveries. You may even end up liking what you initially disliked. Being flexible is especially important as the world is changing so fast that new things are cropping up all the time. This results in many new positions that never existed before.

With the way the new economy is developing, it's inevitable that no matter how good you may be in your profession, you will one-day experience the specter of being laid off or made redundant at one of your jobs. Having a positive attitude will deter you from thinking it's your own fault or inadequacy. Instead, you'll accept that as just one of those things in life that is not within your own control. A good rule of thumb: don't take things personally especially on matters where you have absolutely no say.

Languages

Being multilingual is a definite plus. As English is now the universal business language, you can't expect to get any meaningful work with any major organization in the world without a firm foundation in it. Where you work and live will determine what other languages you will need to have.

For example, in the United States, there's been a big increase in recent years of immigrants from Spanish-speaking countries such as Cuba, Mexico and elsewhere in Latin America. So in certain states such as California, Texas and Florida, where many of them have settled, Spanish has become an official second language. Even for members of the European Union who now share a common currency – the euro – they still each maintain their own language and culture.

Pre-1997, English was Hong Kong's business language. Today, Chinese has become just as important, if not even more so. However, for Hong Kong to retain its competitive edge as a world financial center, it must promote and maintain its bi-lingual — or more accurately now its tri-lingual — tradition. In addition to English, it must also have two of the major Chinese dialects. This is because Hong Kong uses Cantonese, while the mainland has *putonghua*, the national or common language. Also, if Hong Kong aspires to a larger slice of the service-economy pie, such communications skills are crucial.

China, too, would have to follow Hong Kong's lead, if it is serious about its quest to be a major player in the world community of nations. Unlike colonial times when many people can get by without the language skills, if you want to work today in the greater China region, most jobs require working fluency in English and *putonghua*. Obviously, if based in Hong Kong, knowing Cantonese will also be a big plus for both your personal and professional lives.

As there are large pockets of Chinese population in all major cities of the world, knowing some Chinese will enhance your overall prospects no matter where you live. For those of us born Chinese, we should take advantage of our rich cultural heritage by making it a top priority to learn as much as we can about our own history and languages. Having a firm foundation in our own origins will help us to know and understand ourselves better.

To summarize: having some fluency, in major languages such as English, Chinese, Japanese, German, French and Spanish will enhance both your personal and professional prospects. Languages can enrich your life in other ways as well. There's no greater pleasure than to be able to chat with foreign friends in their own language. Learning a foreign language will also get you in touch with that country's culture, history and traditions.

Computer literacy

Obviously the more computer literate you are, the better your prospects will be. But as a minimum, most places now require some knowledge of word processing, spreadsheets and a database, as well as in communications such as e-mail. As all things technical are continuously evolving, a more important consideration is that you're willing and able to learn and keep up with the rapid changes that are taking place. Don't be discouraged or be intimidated by the sound of things. Like everything else, proficiency will come with practice, patience and perseverance.

Inevitably, however, with so much going on, it's impossible to learn everything. So you'll have to set priorities for yourself. Start with the basics and then take one step at a time. It's always handy to know where you can find the instructions to solve some of the common problems that you're apt to encounter from time to time. Instead of practicing on a theoretical level, it's often more constructive to work on a real project. For example, if you need to learn how to use the spreadsheet, why not set up an income and expense statement or an investment portfolio? Or if you need to create a database, why not practice on building your own address book?

Cross disciplines

In a knowledge-based economy, there is an increasing demand for people who can offer a broader spectrum of skills and experience; for example, an engineering, computer science or biology degree combined with one in law, medicine or business administration. In recent years, an increasing number of universities in the United States have been offering multidiscipline degrees. At New York's Columbia University, for example, a student attending the Graduate School of Journalism may also, at the same time, be studying for a master's degree in business administration or international and public affairs. Depending on the program, you may have to spend a bit more time to do this.

While it's crucial to be technology minded and oriented, for the coming decades, it'd be more important to have a broader-based education than just learning exactly which buttons to push and when. The information technology explosion that we're currently experiencing is just the first phase. As this progresses, there will be a convergence of computer, communication and content, eliminating the need for you to learn how to operate the machinery hands on as we must do currently. In the foreseeable future, you may only need to speak to your PC and it will do whatever tasks you ask it to do.

We'll also see a major shift from the current preference for specialists, who cover in some depth a rather narrow area or field, to a growing demand for generalists who are well conversant in a wide variety of disciplines and can pull different events or data together and relate them to each other. That's why even in this Internet age, the old basics such as reading, writing and arithmetic are still as relevant today, if not even more so than ever before. A winning formula for the coming years would be to combine these traditional basics with as wide an exposure as possible to a mix of cultures and disciplines, plus a good dose of technological know-how.

Although high technology will infringe on every facet of our life, it will mean different things in different professions. For those artistically inclined, many of the traditional methods of learning will still be valid. For example, musicians – whether singers or instrumentalists – may use technology, as an aid in their studies, but their main resource remains an enlightening and compatible teacher/mentor. But these teachers are also just human, so what they impart to their students will consist of what they've acquired in their own experience and can often be biased. Keep in mind that in every generalization there are exceptions. In the final analysis, it's only the exceptions that really count.

In the performing arts, as in everything else, it's crucial to avail yourself to as wide an exposure as possible. Being open to learning different techniques from different mentors will help you to develop your own style, maximize your natural talents and minimize your limitations. Mentors are also your best contacts and resources. They will play critical roles in how your future career as a performer will develop.

For the more experienced professionals such as medical doctors and lawyers who decide at mid-career to change professions, this should be a time of great opportunities. Instead of discarding what they spent years learning and practicing, they should take advantage of their accumulated experience and knowledge and build on that.

For example, lawyers who decide they want to be PC experts can easily learn all about computers and programming and then combine these with their legal know-how to specialize in say, privacy laws, as it relates to the Internet — an important area that has yet to be fully explored. With all the major changes in the health-care industry in recent years, doctors can easily combine their medical expertise with a number of other careers including that of hi-tech researcher, business executive, hospital or public health administrator, writer, broadcaster or lobbyist for health issues. For those charitably inclined, there's a host of challenging volunteer work available.

In this fast-moving information-technology environment, all of us must learn to be nimble, ultra observant and to think creatively on a multilateral level.

Learning is for life

Knowledge generates confidence. What you have learned is the only thing in life no one can take away from you. And, you're never too young or too old to learn. To survive in this new economic environment, it's important to take stock of yourself regularly by asking where do you want to go and what skills are necessary? You'll soon discover that the more you learn, the more you need to know. Unless you're willing to continuously explore this fast-evolving world, you'll end up being left behind. The key to staying on top: invest in yourself via continuing education and keep up-to-date with what's going on both near and far.

In short, the more you can offer in terms of knowledge and experience, the more attractive and valuable you will be to a prospective employer. Of course there's a personal benefit to this as well, as being a more fulfilled person will mean a better quality of life for both yourself and for your family. Learning need not be all concentrated just on work prospects. It can be for fun too — a chance to do what you love. The most precious gift that you can leave your children is to instill in them this love and commitment to lifetime learning.

Mastering some economic basics

Mastering a few economic fundamentals will make reading the daily newspapers more interesting. It will help you develop a better understanding of what's happening in the world around you. Following are four basic ideas to get you started.

Everything has its season

In this ever-changing world, it will be to our advantage to understand certain basic facts. First, everything from people to governments to economies exists for a time and goes through cycles with high and low points. These various stages can occur in various places at different times with varying lengths and intensities.

To illustrate, let's take a look at the three major economic regions of the world during the last two decades.

At the dawn of the new millennium, the United States was in top economic shape with low interest rates, inflation and unemployment. Asia, where some countries had phenomenal growth in the last few years, was, however, going through a painful period of economic restructuring, following the 1997 crisis.

Meanwhile, the 12 original European Union [EU] countries have been working overtime to get their houses in order so they can meet the minimum standards needed for monetary union at the start of 1999, when they adopted the euro as their common currency.

The picture in the1970s and early 1980s was quite different:

▶ Two times during that decade, the economies of the world were hit by record high, double-digit interest rates, inflation and unemployment, the result of OPEC [Organization of Petroleum Exporting Countries] oil price wars. Being the largest consumer of energy products, the United States was one of the most affected. As companies there struggled for survival, they resorted to the now familiar twin strategy of cutting costs and restructuring — mostly downsizing — their operations. Although the economy has been back on track for some years now, many U.S. firms are still on this cost-cutting and consolidation wagon.

▶ In Asia, Japan and the Tigers — Hong Kong, Singapore, Taiwan and Korea (commonly also known as the four newly-industrialized countries or NICs) — were just on the verge of taking off to be joined later by neighboring countries such as China, Thailand, Indonesia, Malaysia and the Philippines. Many of these countries prospered and grew during those years at a pace beyond expectations. Major international banks flocked to the region and offered tons of easy money to fuel these heated markets. It was just a matter of time before there would be a big bust. It came in the summer of 1997, starting in Thailand. But even before then, there were already signs that Japan, the second largest economy in the world after the United States, was on the first step of a long-term downward slide.

▶ Europe, too, has its ups-and-downs during this period, culminating in the late 1980s with the fall of the Berlin Wall. Finally, East and West Germany were reunified after having been divided since the end of the Second World War in 1945. Then started a wave of west-to-east transfers of everything from products and services to legal systems. Today, a decade later, the tide has turned and increasingly, eastern systems and ideas are flowing westward.

But for the former West Germany, the cost of supporting its eastern cousins has been a very heavy financial burden. Many westerners were complaining bitterly about what they perceived to be preferential treatment given by their government to the easterners, while they see no end in sight to the tax surcharges that they've been paying the past decade. Meanwhile, the easterners were complaining too, claiming the west was not doing enough for them, as unemployment rose to a record high. So at a recent election, the German people voiced their growing dissatisfaction by rejecting Helmut Kohl, the chancellor for the past 16 years and the leading supporter for unification.

What this brief summary of world economies in the recent past reminds us is that it's in the nature of things that nothing lasts forever. What goes up must eventually come down. Over time, most such cyclical movements will follow a certain pattern. However, because we live in a shrinking world, both in terms of distance and time, we're being inundated with increasingly rapid and volatile changes even as we grow ever more interdependent. Take what happened with the U.S. stock markets during 2000. It started as a charging bull and ended the year a beaten bear. The NASDAQ Composite Index — where most of the new economy hi-tech stocks are listed — plunged 40% with the Blue Chip Dow Jones Industrial Average dropped 6%, compared with a surge of over 85% and 25% respectively for 1999.

As the year 2000 progressed, there were growing signs that the U.S. economy may be in the throes of a slowdown or possibly even a recession. An added uncertainty as we enter 2001 is what the new president, George W. Bush, and his administration will do. This is now being very closely monitored, as what happens in the United States will also affect Asia, Europe and all the places in-between — often at about the same moment now that real-time news is a common way of life.

We are also in the midst of a major crossroads as the new economy battles with the old for supremacy. It's inevitable that the current information technology fever will have great impact on our economy. It's still too soon to tell what new patterns will emerge but what's obvious is that many of the traditional market strategies may no longer be effective in this new environment. If history is any guide, however, chances are we'll see a global convergence of interests ·between the companies of the new economy and those of the old. Competition will be so intense that only the largest and the fittest will manage to survive.

So it is crucial that we keep ourselves informed about trends and the direction of the various cycles in different regions of the world. But keep in mind that nothing remains static. We cannot just apply current information, as is, to future events. A misleading, but common practice is for students to make decisions about their future careers based solely on current job-market outlooks. By the time they graduate, the market could easily have completely reversed itself. There is always a time lag between when forecast surveys are compiled and when they're released to the public. The idea then is not just to be kept well informed, but also to give some thought to what new trends may emerge in the foreseeable future.

There are no free lunches

A second fact of life is that in everything we do, from a financial transaction to giving a helping hand, there are inevitably some tradeoffs. For someone to benefit or gain, another person has to take a risk or to incur a loss. Keeping this fact in mind will help us to be more conscious of the need to analyze and balance the positive and negative influences that may affect our daily dealings, plus what all this could mean to those who are involved.

This is all the more crucial as the popular press, especially personal finance publications, are fond of doing high-profile surveys of the best and worst of a wide range of investments and products. One question they rarely deal with fully is for whom are these the best? Of course, sometimes even the worst can actually be good for someone out there. It all depends on the situation at a particular point in time.

As no two of us are alike in our own profiles, it's often useful to develop an ability to put yourself in another person's place. This way you'll have a clearer understanding of why they behave the way they do. For example, how to allocate limited resources is one issue most of us who have to deal with family budgets readily understand. Most of us, however, would not think of applying the same stringent test when we're faced with public policy issues or special interest group activities such as the environment or human rights. All this costs money and there are only limited resources available. For every free rider, there must always be someone else who pays. As responsible citizens in an open society, we should aim for some balance so there'd be more sharing between those who give and those who take.

This no-free-lunch rule applies even to personal freedom, a privilege more people will enjoy, as a growing number of societies become industrialized. Such political and financial freedom, however, comes with a rising price tag. As the trend accelerates for the three traditional sustaining pillars of our society — families, employers and governments — to play lesser roles in the management of our daily lives, we must now assume increasing responsibility to achieve our own financial independence. In this evolving economic environment, personal financial planning will assume an increasingly important role in our lives in the new millennium.

To survive in this new economy, we must all be taking more responsibility for ourselves. However, this doesn't mean that we have to be completely self-obsessed and forget everyone else. What good is prosperity if we have no one to share it with? If we were to enjoy a high quality of life, we need a caring family and community. Unfortunately, as more of us concentrate increasingly only on selfish pursuits, these two most treasured traditions are sadly being eroded away. As the alternatives are unthinkable, it's time we join hands and work to revert this self-destructive trend.

Supply and demand

A third fact of life: the price we can command for our labor or to pay for goods and services depend largely on the supply and demand in the market place. Generally speaking, when the supply is low and the demand high, prices will rise. It follows that when the supply is high and demand low, prices will begin to drop.

The function of the market then is to provide a medium of transactions between buyers — the demand side — and the sellers — the supply side. This concept applies not just to commercial transactions but also to most every conceivable thing that we may do today. Even colleges and churches must compete to get the type of students or congregants that they want. Understanding this basic concept will help you to plan and organize accordingly. In short, when you're in the market either as a buyer or seller, you must have something to offer — some special talents or products — that will attract some takers. Needless to say, the more you have that's unique to offer, the greater your prospects will be.

For example, if you were a student looking for a college or a job, it'd be more efficient to search for institutions or firms that are involved in interests and disciplines that match your own. Keep in mind: be it a school or a company, you're forming an equal partnership with them. They need you as much as you need them. For any relationship to work, it must be mutually beneficial.

Telling tales with numbers

It's been said that numbers don't lie for there can only be one correct answer to arithmetic questions such as two plus two or ten minus five. May be that's why numbers are often used to keep track of economic activities. But like everything else, numbers have their limitations as well.

Numbers computed under certain situations, for example, may not give as absolute an answer as some people often assume they do. Depending on a variety of factors such as the time frames involved, the items being compared or the points of view being advanced, they may even be open to differing interpretations. As a result, numbers can be easily manipulated or be skewed towards certain stands or viewpoints.

Take stock indices or economic indicators. As they are compiled following a set of varying criteria, the numbers generated tell only about what's included in the calculation and not of the larger universe as a whole. To illustrate, let's take a look at the Wall Street Journal's 103-year-old Dow Jones Industrial Average, a commonly used indicator of how the stock market is faring. Until recently the 30 stocks included in the Dow were all listed on the New York Stock Exchange, which carry a total of some 2000. There are, of course, in addition, thousands of other listed shares on stock exchanges in other cities.

To acknowledge the increasing importance of technology and the decline of manufacturing, the Wall Street Journal recently decided to revise the Dow index to better reflect the current market realities. Effective 1 November 1999, Microsoft, Intel, SBC Communications, a regional phone giant, and Home Depot, a home improvement retailer, replaced Goodyear Tire, Sears Roebuck, Union Carbide and Chevron.

With the addition of Microsoft and Intel, it's the first time that the average carries any NASDAQ over-the-counter shares. Although these changes will make the Dow more representative, looking at it alone will still give a rather narrow view of the market as a whole.

Knowing the components of an index or an indicator will help us see its limitations and to understand better what it's supposed to cover or not cover. Here again, we'll have to look at a number of different ones before we'll be able to come up with a complete picture. Also, be sure that what's being compared are actually similar in every respect. For example, when comparing the track records of fund managers, be sure to look at numbers that are from the same periods. Otherwise, their results may vary greatly.

As numbers are a big part of business and economic news coverage in our daily life, there's no way to escape from them even if you, like many, may find numbers threatening or simply boring. But they need not be, as numbers can be a very useful tool for you. Mastering some of the basic indicators to which the market attaches a high level of importance will help you immensely in sorting out and analyzing what you read or hear in the news every day.

As the United States is the largest economy, what happens there is being closely followed and monitored around the world. To get you started in learning more about these key indicators, listed below are six key economic figures that are released there on a regular basis. Most, if not all, countries also publish similar categories of economic data, although some may be more accurate than others. No matter where you live, chances are your local media will carry data that pertain to your region, plus a selection from the major economies, including the United States, Japan and Germany.

▶ **Interest rates** — Interest is the cost of using money. It's expressed as a rate for a certain period of time, say, one year, commonly known as the annual rate of interest. A key interest rate to watch is the prime rate, the rate banks charge to their most trustworthy customers, normally the blue-chip companies. Loans to less well-established firms and to individuals are often tied to the prime rate. For example, a preferred customer may borrow at a prime rate of 8%, but an ordinary one may have to pay prime plus 2%, for a total of 10%. What determines the prime rate are the market forces that affect a bank's cost of funds and the rates that borrowers will accept.

Interest rates play an important role in the financial health of both businesses and individuals. Whether this is good or bad depends largely on which side of the fence you happen to be on. When rates are high, interest-sensitive industries such as insurance or utilities companies will fare badly. For consumers seeking high returns on their savings, high rates are a bonanza. But for those who need to borrow, especially for long-term loans such as home mortgages, high interest could keep them out of the market. When rates are low, the reverse would be true. So companies and individuals can borrow cheaply but pensioners will suffer as their bank savings will earn lower returns and reduce their income.

▶ **The U.S. dollar** — For the United States, the strong performance of its currency in recent years carries both a blessing and a curse. For Americans who travel abroad, a strong dollar makes their trips cheaper. For the U.S. economy, however, it has increased its trade deficit to record levels as a strong dollar makes it costlier for foreign companies to trade with America, resulting in more goods being imported than exported.

For firms or individuals who invest overseas, the possibility is always present that the eventual currency conversion back to the dollar may cancel out all the gains. For countries such as Hong Kong whose currency is pegged to the U.S. dollar, whatever happens state-side may eventually also have some similar direct impacts on their local economies.

▶ **Consumer price index** [CPI] — Also known as the cost-of-living index, this measures the price change in a fixed basket of goods on a month-over-month basis. Compiled by the U.S. Bureau of Labor Statistics, updates are released usually during the second week of the month, covering the previous month. The major components in the index include the costs of housing, food, transportation and electricity. A sub-category, *all items excluding food and energy*, carries a great deal of weight, as it is considered to represent a core rate of inflation.

A high inflation rate diminishes spending power and reduces an investment's total returns. That is why, when looking at total returns, it's a good idea to factor in the inflation rate. For example, if a 30-year U.S. Treasury bond yields 6% and inflation is at 3%, the real return is 3%. Today, many U.S. employment contracts and pensions are tied to the changes in the CPI as protection against inflation and reduced purchasing power.

Deflation, the reverse of inflation, can be just as unhealthy for your pocketbook as a high inflation rate. Note: don't confuse deflation with disinflation, which is a slowing down in the rate of price increases. While inflation may, or may not, stimulate output and employment, marked deflation has always caused unemployment to rise and output to fall.

▶ **Employment** — Released by the U.S. Bureau of Labor Statistics on the first Friday of each month covering the previous month, economists use this data to forecast other economic indicators due out later in the month. So the market attaches a very high, if not the highest level of importance to this survey. The two most important categories are the *unemployment rate* and the change in *non-farm payroll*. Other important sub-categories in this report are *manufacturers' total hours worked* and *hourly wages*.

If unemployment drops too low it may signal to the market that there's more demand than supply so wages will rise accordingly. If this continues without some balance, it may trigger a higher inflation rate and diminish consumer-spending power. That is why sometimes the financial markets react positively when unemployment is on the high side and reacts negatively when it's low. Needless to say, for the workers, the exact opposite would be true.

▶ **Gross domestic product [GDP]** — The GDP covers the total value of goods and services produced in a nation. It replaced the gross national product as the Commerce Department's main measure of U.S. economic output. The GDP measures all goods and services produced by both American and non-American workers in the United States. There are four categories: personal consumption, investment, government spending and net exports. Annual GDP figures are released quarterly with monthly revisions.

▶ **Gross national product [GNP]** — The GNP covers the total value of goods and services produced in the United States, including those the nation produces abroad. Annual GNP figures are released quarterly, as is an inflation-adjusted version, called the real GNP.

A crucial point to keep in mind when dealing with these economic indicators is that markets trade on expectations. That is, what the market place forecasted as the expected levels often carry more weight than the actual data released in each survey. In short, the wider the difference between the actual and their expected results, the more the potential impact on market prices. This is why a great deal of economic and business news coverage is often given to forecasting what these indicators and corporate earnings may look like in the coming months or years.

Managing life on your own

Unless you went away to school, having a first job is often the time when you'll move out of your parents' home. Managing life on your own requires coping with life's many demands and stresses. This juggling is not only of financial resources but also of your time as well. Don't be infected by the workaholic bug — a common affliction in the modern work place. An efficient worker is a well-rounded person who also plays hard and indulges in other interests or hobbies.

Traditionally, most people's lives are closely tied to their work places especially in company towns. Often friends, relatives, including husbands and wives, all work for the same company. But for sometime now, this picture of continuity, company loyalty and community has been evolving. As these changes take hold, job security as we know it today, will become obsolete.

Instead of having one job for life in one spot, most workers may have to migrate from job to job at different locations. Although greater mobility will bring more opportunities, it's no guarantee of job satisfaction. That's why it's important to develop other interests that would give you a sense of purpose. The loss of community means many people will end up leading more isolated lives. Among these changes, there will also be a distinct separation between your professional and personal life, as the private and public sectors tackle the growing need to develop better work ethics and conflict of interest policies. To prevent both being laid off at the same time, husbands and wives should probably avoid working for the same employer in this new environment.

How to monitor your own progress

To ensure you're working towards the right direction, it's a good idea to develop a simple system to monitor your own progress.

The simplest is to make two checklists — one for work and the other for your personal life — listing a few simple goals, covering varying time frames. For example, on the work list, the short-term ones may include building contacts and networking sources; the longer-term ones to work on could be what your next job should be or what you may want to study that will lead you to the next step on the ladder. Be specific and set a deadline.

Do the same with the personal list. If you just moved to a new town or city, you may want to set aside time to meet new friends, try the best restaurants or attend some of the cultural offerings. For the longer term, you may want to furnish your flat, plan for a holiday overseas, start a new hobby, save money to buy your own home, go to graduate school or get married.

As with any lists, you should check them periodically and update them accordingly. Here's a simple form to get you started.

Pauline Tai

Personal Goals			
Long Term		**Follow up**	
Date	**Description**	**Date**	**Comments**
Date	**Short Term**	**Date**	**Comments**

Work Goals

Date	Long Term Description	Follow up Date	Comments

Date	Short Term	Date	Comments

4. Think Ahead

What better time to start learning how to think on multilevels than right now by giving some thought to four areas — education, career, personal finance and personal family history — that will play critical roles in the quality of your future life? How well you know yourself will be the key to how successful you will be in dealing with these life-long issues. Keep in mind that how you handle these will affect not just you personally but will also have great impact on how you will deal with your own children in the foreseeable future.

It's a fact of life that nothing ever gets accomplished unless there's a plan. Constructing a workable plan, however, requires some creative thinking and knowledge. Why is it that some people are creative while others simply lack any imagination at all? Is creativity innate or can it be learned? These are intriguing questions with no definitive answers. But we do know that having a plan is just the first step. It takes practical action to turn the plan into reality. Traditionally, most idea people are often labeled as dreamers and thus are considered not as adept as doers or vice versa. To cope in the new economy, however, we'll have to do a better job of nurturing both our imagination and our sense of pragmatism.

As human beings are creatures of habit, chances are what we picked up when young — whether good or bad — will stay with us for the rest of our lives. That is why it's so crucial to develop sound habits right from the start. Our attitudes and behavior are influenced and molded by the values and cultures of our families and the communities where we originated or lived. Studies have shown that when children from abusive families become parents, they're more likely to treat their own offspring in the same violent manner as they have once experienced themselves.

If something is of interest to us, we'd be willing to spend time to learn about it. Also, we'd do a better job if it were something that we like and enjoy. However, such interests don't develop in a void. They have to be somehow sparked through exposure to the universe around us. Our very first contact with the world is through our parents, their families and friends, as well as with the population and institutions in our communities such as schools and religious institutions. If, for example, our parents love books and music, chances are we will also be so inclined. By being exposed to a wider world, we'll have a chance to develop more interests, resulting in more opportunities being made available to us later on.

Unfortunately, many families and school systems today are in such dire dysfunctional states that they're creating more problems and harm to their young than helping and nurturing them. How can parents and teachers be role models to their children if they themselves were not prepared to handle the new realities? As a result, many students are left to struggle on their own without the proper guidance or attention that they must have if they are to develop properly.

In former times, not so very long ago, when life was simpler, most people tended to follow a rather predictable and structured route. They were expected to perform certain duties at different stages of their life. For example, they'd go to school, graduate, take a job, marry, have children and retire. But with the new economy these stages are not as clearly marked or defined any more. For some time now they have been evolving into an on-going process. We, in effect, just keep adding more stages, which results in generating ever more options and choices. Ideally, we should make it a lifelong goal to allow ourselves both the time to experience new things and to indulge in what we really want to do.

With increasing demands on our limited time, its crucial we develop the habit of setting priorities with varying time frames for ourselves. Be sure to include a mix of long-term and short-term goals, plus a smattering in-between. While thinking of the future, don't forget to take advantage and allocate some time to enjoy the present as well.

Let's start by taking a quick look at the four areas – education and career, personal finance and personal history record keeping — that deserve our fullest attention. If we can master them, we'll be that much closer to achieving a certain level of competence in managing our own lives in the new economy. To do justice to these topics, three separate volumes will be released in the coming months. Although the four volumes of this series are closely interrelated, each book is a complete entity by itself and can be read separately or chronologically. Even the chapters are self-contained so they can be treated like individual articles in a magazine. The choice then is entirely up to the individual reader's own interest at any particular point in time.

Pauline Tai

Education

Plato was right when he said that education is wasted on the young, for most of us really don't much appreciate our days in school. But the fact remains that for an increasing number of people, the first 20 years or more of life is spent on education of one sort or another. Unfortunately, a growing number of students are not taking proper advantage of their years in school. A majority don't really know why they're there or what's expected of them – never mind about what they want to do either there or later on. So they often simply while their time away or study disciplines that mean little to them except possibly those were easy courses that require a minimum of effort from them.

Depending where you live and how your school system is organized, most students in lower schools don't really have much choice but to take whatever curriculums are available. Some systems have very rigid requirements while others give students a free range. Obviously all these methods have flaws as the whole concept of one-size fits all is in itself flawed. Ideally lower schools should be the first place where we're exposed to as wide a range of the world around us as possible. But if we're allowed to pick and choose, chances are we'd take the easier paths and refrain from taking too many chances.

We should be open to ideas as how else do we find out where our own interests may lie? Through exposure and experience we get to develop a sense of our own likes and dislikes. Going to school or college is a bit like being on an apprenticeship. The more you can learn during those years, the higher the quality of life you'll be able to attain later on.

Traditionally, parents and other family members also play a very key role in our education. But with the advent of the nuclear family where often both parents work, the burden of educating the young have fallen almost solely on our teachers. Unfortunately, most school systems really don't have the necessary qualified personnel or resources to cope efficiently and effectively with this situation. For parents who could spend time with their children, they too often feel inadequate in their ability to guide them through the ever-changing maze.

Maybe parents and children should join forces and work as a team rather than as opposing contenders, as many companies are now encouraging their employees to do with their employers. Here again the key to success is a good channel of communication where on-going constructive discussions are encouraged and differing opinions are treated with mutual respect. If we'd only listen with an open mind, there are always things that we can learn from each other. Often just listening to what people say is not enough. We must also listen to why they are saying it.

Career

If you must work, you might as well do something you like and enjoy. A career, after all, may last 40 or more years. Chances are this will be spread over at least half a dozen or more different positions at as many organizations. Keep in mind that your first jobs are in reality just apprenticeships. Unless you're the lucky few who gained practical work experience while studying, most graduates who enter the job market must spend six months to a year or more being trained and becoming proficient in their positions. It's not unusual to find that after this tryout, you may decide that's not really what you want to do.

One easy way to help yourself is to start thinking about careers earlier while still in school. Needless to say, the younger you begin, the more time you'll have to explore the possibilities. One way to learn about what's out there is to take an interest in what others do. How many children really know what their parents do to make a daily living? Start with your parents. Don't be afraid to ask questions. If possible, arrange to go with them to work one day. See for yourself. Get a feel of the environment, the work they do and their colleagues. Other relatives, friends and teachers are also good sources for such job tips.

High school or college students can seek out companies that offer summer internships in fields that are of interest to you. If, for example, you're thinking of becoming a journalist, you can check out media companies such as Dow Jones or The South China Morning Post to see what internship programs they're offering to students. Depending on the sponsoring firm, most of these programs will pay a small stipend to cover expenses. But money is really not the key here. It's the experience that would count most.

Doing an internship provides you with a great opportunity to work inside one of these companies, meet some people in the industry and gain invaluable first-hand experience that would stand you in good stead later on. To give you as wide a perspective as possible, often you'll be given a chance to rotate between a number of different jobs. If nothing else, being there will confirm for you whether that's what you'd really want to take on as a career.

As workers in the new economy, we will have to get used to the idea that no matter how good we may be in our chosen field, at some point, we may be laid off or made redundant as the result of company restructuring or some other changes. As long as you've done the best job you know how, you have nothing to be ashamed of. So don't take it personally. Being able to talk about it openly with your family and friends will also make the transition less painful. It's best to move on rather than wasting precious time over something that's not within your control. Most times, things do happen for the best. Attitudes and how you look at things often affect how they will turn out in the end.

Pauline Tai

Personal finance

The recent proliferation of personal finance coverage is very much a story of our times, the result of the rapid advancements in technology, market innovations and deregulation in the 1980s. As globalization and digital technology take hold in the 1990s, these processes are accelerating at an even faster pace. In such a super-charged and uncertain environment, where speed and volatility will increasingly haunt the world's financial markets, personal finance is destined to play an ever more critical role in the new millennium.

Personal finance coverage is so common today it's hard to believe the first publication to deal with this topic on a regular basis made its debut in the United States only in 1972, when Time Inc. started Money magazine. During those early days, Money's coverage concentrated mostly on consumer issues and products. A gradual shift from consumerism to investing and personal financial occurred during the first oil crisis in 1974, when skyrocketing interest rates and inflation played havoc with the world economies. When the cold war ended in the late 1980s, personal finance's position was firmly established, as economics and trade replace geopolitics as the major point of contention among nations.

Today, Money has a host of competitors to contend with including Dow Jones-Hearst's Smart Money, Kiplinger's Personal Finance Magazine and Worth. Major newspapers around the country have also expanded their business coverage to include special sections on personal finance. In fact, personal finance has become such a hot topic that even traditional business publications such as The Wall Street Journal, Business Week and Fortune are now devoting special sections and/or issues to this topic.

As financial deregulation expands to other countries, personal finance coverage is now also beginning to appear regularly in major cities of the world. The rapid growth of e-commerce and trading on the Internet has also helped to spawn an increasing number of on-line businesses and financial newsletters that deal with personal finance issues.

For consumer-investors then, it's now not a matter of insufficient information, but one of having too much and often of questionable quality. There's a tendency in personal finance coverage to generalize, oversimplify and exaggerate, as, for example, giving advice on the best or worst of this or that investment or products without answering the crucial question of for whom; or when the stories themselves do not live up to the sensational headlines. It's all the more ironic as personal finance deals with individuals and as no two of them are ever exactly alike, what's good for one person, may actually be bad for the next. So here again unless you have a good handle on your own temperament and risk threshold, this type of hype can often mislead you. Note: even if you can afford the services of a professional money manager, his role is to advise and suggest. You are still responsible for making the final decisions.

58

As your own future financial security depends to a large extend on how efficiently you're able to monitor and manage your own personal finance, it's to your advantage to spend a little time to familiarize yourself with the tools that you'll need to handle this job properly and efficiently. As the name "personal finance" implies, it's personal on one end and financial on the other. The first part requires you to get a clear picture of yourself — your own character and temperament, likes and dislikes, risk threshold, goals and so on. The second covers the financial universe that includes the what, how, why, when and where of the products and the professionals that you may have to deal with along the way. Having some firm foundation in both these areas will help you make sounder decisions and select investments that will meet your own personal profile and requirements.

Achieving some level of financial independence will help tide you over when and if you should be laid off or when you want to take a break for whatever reason, including returning to school, taking a trip around the world or staying home to care for your new baby. Contrary to popular myth, you don't need tons of money to accomplish these goals. What it takes is some thoughtful, advance planning, a strong commitment and a good dose of discipline and patience. The basics of personal finance will be discussed in details in the third volume of this four-part self-development series.

Personal-family history

As we journey through life's many adventures, we learn, we toil, we love and we add to our experiences. But at the same time, we're also acquiring an unending collection of IDs, PINS, passwords, dates, addresses, accounts and whatever else – all the trimmings of a bureaucratic electronic world that often reduces human beings to a long series of characters and numbers. Most of us are often searching for tidbits of such practical data that are needed to complete some official forms or statements such as for school, work, hospital, travel visas or immigration applications. Some questions are so historical that we may have to consult family members for the answers.

With increased mobility, many families today are scattered around the world. Unless we make a special effort to keep in touch, it is inevitable the younger generations will know little or nothing about their forebears or background. It is with this in mind that a fourth volume is included in this series as the personal-family history manager.

When you have completed this workbook, especially the personal section, you will have an up-to-date record of your life, including a medical history of your immediate family. This last is especially useful, as it will make you more aware of what you may face one day in your own health   Next time you are at the doctor's or are called upon to fill in a form, you will have all the important facts at your fingertip. For future generations, your data book will also give them an invaluable source of information about their own origin and background. Needless to say, the earlier you start writing in this book, the easier it will be to keep up-to-date your own life story.

5. Get Help

When embarking on any projects, knowing where to get the right information is half the battle. With the Internet this task is made both easier and more complex. There's a great deal more out there to choose from but quantity alone does not guarantee quality. Just surfing and fishing around in that vast ocean of data can be a time-consuming and, in many countries, an expensive operation, as the time spent on-line is being charged by the minute. Besides, getting the information is only the first step. It's what you do with this information that is the key. Information, like talking, is no substitute for action.

Before you start doing the actual research on any topic – say, where to go to school — it's a good idea to first make an outline of what it is that you're trying to achieve. Start with a list of your own personal preferences such as what it is that you'd like to study, where you'd like to go that and so on. Then take a look at the broader picture of the places that you've chosen. It's a good idea to include your own home country plus at least three or four other choices so you can make some sound comparisons between them.

Once you've had a good handle on this larger universe, then you can zero in on the specific schools that you feel will meet your requirements.

You'll find some of the best tips will come from people you can speak with and ask questions. Start with those nearest you such as your parents, relatives and teachers. School and public libraries can also be good sources, as are embassies, consulates and trade or tourist information services of the countries of your choice.

Following are some useful sources to get you started on further study and research in the topics discussed in this volume.

General	What's Available
Amazon.com www.amazon.com	Books, calendars, CDs, videos, tapes and much more
Barnes and Noble www.barnesandnoble.com	Books, calendars, CDs, videos, tapes and much more
Business Week www.businessweek.com	A weekly covering business that's available by subscription or at newsstands.
The Economist www.economist.com	A financial weekly that originated from London, available in most major cities at newstands or by subscription.
Far Eastern Economic Review www.feer.com	Another member of the Dow Jones family, this weekly is based in Hong Kong.
The Financial Times www.ft.com	A daily available in most major cities at newsstands or by subscription.
Microsoft NBC www.msnbc.com	General and business news, quotes, plus other financial related information.
The New York Times www.nytimes.com	New York City's morning newspaper with the slogan "All the news that's fit to print."
South China Morning Post www.scmp.com	Hong Kong's major English daily
The Wall Street Journal www.wsj.com	This U.S. financial daily also publishes an Asian and European edition. Its interactive edition is one of the few publications that have succeeded in gaining a substantial number of paying on-line subscribers.
The Washington Post www.washingtonpost.com	Washington D.C.'s major newspaper.
Yahoo www.yahoo.com	This is one of the major search engines.

Education	What's Available
American College Testing Program www.collegeapps.about.com	General information about sources of financial aid and how to apply for it, plus help in filing a family financial statement to find out how much aid you can expect to get toward college expenses.
College Board www.collegeboard.org	Provides general information on financial aid and college and university costs; also steers applicants to advanced-placement courses and exams, including a state-by-state list of colleges offering early-decision programs.
Kaplan www.kaplan.com	Offers test preparation and tutoring on college entrance such as SAT, PSAT and ACT that are required for admission to U.S. colleges and universities. Also publishes, with Newsweek, annual guides on How to get into College and How to get into Graduate School.
Peterson's www.petersons.com	Offers a wide range of planning resources for colleges and universities; plus a rundown on early-decision programs.
The Experiment in International Living www.experiment.org.	Information about spending time abroad studying and staying with a host family; this is a great way to experience first hand how other people live and to learn their language and culture.
Smart Student Guide www.finaid.com	Provides information about scholarships, education grants and other financial aids that are available.
US College Application Forms www.weapply.com	Application forms for entry to colleges or universities.

Career	What's Available
Monster Board..Job/resume www.monster.com	Information on the high-tech job markets and what openings are available in those fields
Resume Search www.searchease.com	Recruiting and job market listing
The Rosen Publishing Group, Inc. 29 East 21st Street New York, NY 10010 (800) 237-9932	Rosen specializes in publishing books for young readers. It has a Career series exploring a large number of professions from accounting, firefighting, and medicine to cyberspace, rock music and trucking.
U.S. Department of Labor's Occupation Handbook http://stats.bls.gov/ocohome.htm	An encyclopedic volume listing the various categories of jobs in all major industries, what education and training they require and some brief comments about market outlook for these positions.

Personal Finance	What's Available
American Association of Individual Investors www.aaii.com	A nonprofit education group; an annual membership will entitle you to various publications, such as a bi-monthly on Computerized Investing. In additional, videos on various investment topics, seminars and study groups at reduced costs given in a number of U.S. cities.
Benchmark Investment Funds of Asia www.benchmag.com	A monthly that was recently taken over by the Reader's Digest Association Far East Ltd.
Kiplinger Online www.kiplinger.com	Formerly known as Changing Times, this is the on-line version of its monthly magazine covering topics of interest to the consumer from cars to computers, stocks, bonds, mutual funds to taxes.
Money www.money.com	Part of the Time family of magazines, this is their monthly personal finance magazine.
Errold Moody Jr. efmoody.com	A virtual library of about 1,000 pages of financial information, links, financial quizzes, and investment calculators and advice given by a financial planner and former University of California professor.
Quicken quicken.com	A message board for financial and tax advice staffed by practitioners specializing in these fields.
Smart money www.smartmoney.com	A personal finance magazine started by Dow Jones and the Hearst Magazines.
Worth www.worth.com	Another personal finance magazine
Yahoo www.quote.yahoo.com	You can get quotes of shares as well as other investment information here.

Pauline Tai

Index

Pauline Tai
ptaibooks@yahoo.com

Dear Friend,

RE: New Economy Self-development Series
Volume I: Life in a Rapidly Changing World

If you've arrived at this page, chances are you have just finished reading this book. I hope you enjoyed it, as much as I did writing it for you. In an effort to serve you better in the future, I'd like to hear from you. For your convenience, the few questions below will get you started.

I appreciate your interest and look forward to establishing an on-going interactive dialogue with you.

TO: Pauline Tai   ptaibooks@yahoo.com

FROM: _____   e-mail: _____

Address: _____   Tel: _____

_____   Fax: _____

RE: New Economy Self-development Series
     Volume I: Life in a Rapidly Changing World

1. What is your overall impression of this first volume of a four-part new
    economy self-development series?
    a. Do you find it helpful? _____
    b. What areas would you like to see expanded? _____
    c. Are there any other topics that you'd like to
        see included? _____

2. Who brought this book to your attention? (check one that apply)
    a. Self _____
    b. Relative _____
    c. Teacher _____
    d. Friend _____
    e. Others _____

3. Where did you get this book? (In e-book or paperback?)
    a. Bookstore_____
    b. School or university library _____
    c. Web sites – e-publisher _____
    d. Others _____

4. What is your impression of the overall layout of the book?
   a. Do you like the design and format of
      the book?   _____
   b. Are things laid out clearly?   _____
   c. Do you find it easy to use?   _____

5. The easy practical style of the series was my attempt to involve you, the reader, in a one-to-one basis with me. Do you think I have succeeded in conveying that message? If yes, how can we make it even better? If not, what can we do to improve it?
   a. Yes   _____
   b. No   _____

6. I'm currently working on the remaining volumes of this series that will cover education and career, personal financial planning and a personal family history manager. Will you be interested in these topics?   Why?

   _____
   _____
   _____

7. Would periodic updates on the topics covered in these books be helpful to you? If so, what particular areas are of special interest to you?

   _____
   _____
   _____

8. Other comments:

   _____
   _____
   _____

About the Author

Pauline Tai, born in Guangzhou, China, was raised in Hong Kong and that exotic blend of eastern and western civilization was an abiding influence, which shaped her whole outlook on life.

After university in the United States, Ms. Tai worked as a financial journalist at major publications such as The Wall Street Journal and Money Magazine in New York and the Dow Jones Newswires in Hong Kong. Today she spends part of each year in both cities writing about her favorite topics. At home in five languages, she travels extensively and enjoys keeping in touch with her roots.

Between reporting assignments, she has also taken time out to study and teach at Columbia University in New York City − first as a fellow in the Knight-Bagehot Fellowship for Economics and Business Journalism and later its director. Founded in 1975, this is an intensive year-long program of instruction in economics and business for working mid-career financial journalists.

In addition to her four-part *New Economy Self-Development Series*, her *Chinese Family Cookbook* will also be released in the coming months. A contributor to *Writing about Business: The New Columbia Knight-Bagehot Guide to Economics and Business Journalism* [Columbia University Press, 2001] and *The Columbia Knight-Bagehot Guide to Economics and Business Journalism* [Columbia University Press, 1991], she is also the author of *Mastering Money Matters* [Prentice Hall/Simon & Schuster, 1988] and *The Bachelorette Cookbook* [Doubleday, 1968].

Ms. Tai has also worked at the United Nations in New York in the Office of the Secretary-General. While there, she was also on loan to work on the Conference on New Sources of Energy, in Rome, Italy, and the Conference on Science and Technology in Geneva, Switzerland.

Printed in the United States
6531

9 780759 615366